AN INTROVERT'S GUIDE
TO WORLD DOMINATION

AN
Introvert's
GUIDE TO
WORLD
DOMINATION

BECOME A HIGH LEVEL NETWORKER
AND UPGRADE YOUR LIFE

NICK SHELTON

HOUNDSTOOTH
PRESS

AN INTROVERT'S GUIDE TO WORLD DOMINATION
Become a High Level Networker and Upgrade Your Life

ISBN   978-1-5445-1568-7 *Hardcover*

978-1-5445-1567-0 *Paperback*

978-1-5445-1566-3 *Ebook*

Dedicated to Lucy Nathanson

Thank you for being my North Star, keeping me moving in the right direction.

CONTENTS

INTRODUCTION...9

1. THE JOURNEY......................................13

2. SET UP FOR SUCCESS........................ 33

3. MAKING CONNECTIONS 57

4. NETWORKING 95

5. CONNECTING WITH A HEADLINER/VIP 137

6. NETWORKING IN THE WORKPLACE 149

7. FOLLOW-UP EVENTS...........................175

8. MAINTAINING RELATIONSHIPS..........185

9. THE BIG REVIEW 223

ACKNOWLEDGMENTS............................ 229

ABOUT THE AUTHOR.............................231

INTRODUCTION

Welcome! You're reading the book of an incredibly flawed individual who is alone (by choice) 90 percent of the time and goes to bed around 8 p.m. However, when around people, I have been known to occasionally be awesome and, from time to time, have the opportunity to do some pretty cool stuff. That's what this book is about. I'm going to show you exactly how I built a high-level, strong, close, international network of friends, colleagues, and associates while still remaining an introvert and how you can do the same. This will allow you to upgrade your life substantially along all lines just as I have.

I'd like to start by saying *thank you* so much for purchasing this book and deciding to take action on your life. I guarantee you will be very happy with your results if you simply put in the work. Nothing ever happens until you do the work. I'm here with you, and I'll be here every step of the way. When you're ready to be known, noticed, invited, included, and respected, you've got to start somewhere, and that somewhere is right here—right now.

My mission is to break down this process into digestible pieces and give you a no-nonsense, step-by-step plan to follow. I can tell you this: it's not easy, but it's simple. I'm going to give you everything you need to get out there and excel in social situations.

You'll be developing skills that will give you a great foundation and an outstanding advantage. The techniques you will learn are timeless and designed to get you a "seat at the table" in life.

I know you might be a little nervous about diving into social situations, but I ask for your attention and an open mind. I will lay it out for you. Yes, I know introverts come in many different types, and you most likely are a bit different from me. I'm showing you exactly what worked for me and changed my life. It's your duty to go through these lessons, use what works for you, and discard the rest or save it for another time when it might come in handy.

Do it for yourself, do it for me, do it for the kids—or whatever!—just do it, and you will see results very quickly. All you have to do is just follow the step-by-step plan, and everything will pan out better than you ever expected.

Relationships of all kinds are important, and when you see the power of the connections you make, you will be able to overcome any obstacle life throws your way, because someone in your circle will know about and/or have experience in how to solve whatever problem you are dealing with.

You are only one person, or "connection," away from stepping into your destiny and living a better life—a life that you've wanted but didn't know how to get until now.

So, if you're ready, let's get started.

Thank you very much. Let's do this.

Chapter One

THE JOURNEY

It begins.

I'm the youngest of two sons born to a corporate attorney and a housewife-turned-businesswoman, raised in the sleepy suburbs of anywhere America. When I was seven, my family moved from Houston, Texas, to Littleton, Colorado.

New environment, new people, and a new school.

What do I do? How do I fit in? How do I make new friends?

I remember very clearly my technique. Pick out one kid and talk with them and only them. My friend that first day was a kid named Brenden who was also new. So, I only spoke to him and nobody else. This included teachers—I wasn't big on speaking with adults because I took that whole "don't talk to strangers" thing very seriously.

The teachers thought I might be hearing-impaired. I can't explain the reasoning behind that conclusion, but I ended up in the deaf kids' class.

It was actually pretty cool. There were four of us in there, Patty, Ingrid, Isaac, and myself. It was an intimate setting and I didn't have to talk so I enjoyed it. I made quick friends, played interesting games, and learned sign language.

The good times were not destined to last. Within a few days, my mother found out and made it clear that I was quite capable of hearing and should be put back in "general population" with the rest of the kids. That was a sad day for me. Welcome to the jungle, baby!

HIGH SCHOOL

I had my rag-tag group of friends. We all were a bit socially awkward and anxious, living on the edge of the social groups. It was like the land of misfit toys. We understood each other, or at least we understood enough. But I still felt like I was on the outside looking in.

Not feeling seen can take you to some dark places sometimes. If someone had told me that I was from another planet, and that was the reason why I was so different and had trouble relating to others, I would have believed it. *Where are the others? The others like me? Am I alone?*

There was a very beautiful girl in my English class, a couple rows over. I wanted to ask her out and perhaps get a little bit of...validation.

This was back before you could text people. I'm a bit jealous of folks these days who get to ask people out by text. Impersonal, but easy. I had to call the house of the girl's *parents* and ask to speak with her, and *then* actually have a conversation.

With shaky, sweaty hands, I punched in the numbers on the keypad and held my breath as the phone began to ring.

> Her: Hello.

> Me: May I please speak to...[girl]

> Her: This is she.

> Me: Hey! It's Nick Shelton from English class, how's it going?

> Her: Who?

> Me: Nick Shelton from your English class.

> Her: I don't know a Nick Shelton from English class.

Uh oh, this isn't going well, but I'm already in the mix so let's keep pressing forward.

Me: I'm the black guy two rows over.

Her: There's no black guy in my English class.

Now it occurs to me that I must have been really good at blending in if she didn't even know that there is exactly one black guy in her English class. Me.

Me: I don't even know what to say now.

Her: Is this a joke?

Me: I wish it was.

Her: How'd you get my number?

It's always a bad sign when a girl asks you how you got her number.

Me: A friend gave it to me. Anyway, I was wondering if you would like to go out sometime?

Her: No thank you, Nick Shelton, from English class, I'm going to pass.

Me: All right, have a great night!

Her: Bye.

So...what did I learn? Well, I learned that I really wasn't looking forward to going back to English class. That was going to suck.

I also learned that, apparently, I was so unremarkable that I could be the only black guy in the classroom and still go unnoticed. It became clear that I had to find a solution—a way out.

People should at least know that I exist. I want to be seen. I want to matter.

But how exactly does someone do that?

COLLEGE

I came out of the gate strong. College is a new environment where you can shed the old you and be whatever you want to be, right? I met a few people who were extroverted and figured if I spent time around them, some of that magic would rub off on me.

It worked when I was with them, out on the town with them, in their presence.

It didn't work if I was alone or with people who did not have that trait.

I reverted to my default setting and faded once again into the shadows. But things were a little different. I had gotten a taste of how it could be. How could I get there and stay there? What was the trick?

I thought, *MONEY*. Perhaps if I could just make some money, I would feel more confident, I would be able to talk to anyone I wanted, and people would want to talk with ME. I would be included and invited, and things would just fall into place. I just had to make some moolah.

I started trading commodity futures and was good at it. I got myself a fancy car and a swanky apartment in the cool part of town. And there I was, alone. I had nicer stuff, but I was the exact same guy, a richer version of the same shy introvert. No social scene, no invites to high-end parties—nothing that I imagined it would be.

Unfortunately, or fortunately, the good financial times did not last long. As any commodity futures trader can tell you, most people, sooner or later, lose their shirts in the commodities game, and I was no exception. At twenty years old, I declared bankruptcy.

If you think it's challenging working on your social skills as a quiet fly on the wall, try doing it fresh off bankruptcy!

Next, I tried alcohol, the universal social lubricant.

It did make it easier to talk to people, for sure, but I had to be drinking all the time. If I met someone when I was drinking, and then saw them again when I was sober, they would wonder what was wrong with me. Often, I wouldn't even remember meeting them.

You hear about people crying themselves to sleep. Not me.

Every night before I went to sleep, I would pray.

I would pray to God to please take my life in the night.

I'd had enough. I did not want to continue. Every night, before bed, this was my ritual.

And every morning I would wake up and cry because my prayer went unanswered.

It felt like my soul was torn, and I didn't know how to fix it.

But still, I would head out into another day, broken.

THE MILITARY

I decided to do what a lot of other young broken people do. I joined the military. I wanted the structure; I wanted the discipline. I looked at it as taking a long vacation away from myself and my reality.

My choice was the Air Force. And it was good to me. In its structure and discipline, I found clarity.

The military takes complicated tasks and breaks them into simple steps so that anyone can do them. This applied to everything from folding a shirt to setting up a flight-line fueling operation. It dramatically simplified my life. I began applying these same systems to everything. Take the task, reverse-engineer it, break it down into simple steps, execute.

I believe a superpower within introverts is the power of observation. I began to go out often, mostly alone, but sometimes with people who were good at socializing. I would just quietly observe. I would sit and watch a room, taking in the social dynamics, see what was working and what wasn't. I'd watch the ebb and flow of people mingling.

I started to notice patterns. I took those patterns and then adjusted them because I needed something that would work with my personality style. I wanted to develop a system where being shy or introverted could be a strength. A system where you didn't have to become something else, but where you simply had to leverage what you already were.

So, I applied the military approach to the art of navigating social situations, broke it down into simple steps, then tested it. I adjusted and tested again, adjusted and tested again. I was scoring quick victories, making good connections, and building strong relationships. This encouraged me to keep pushing forward. The system kept getting better, and I kept getting better by using it.

Life was good. The Air Force introduced me to international travel. I was stationed in North Carolina and then Japan; from there I had the opportunity to travel to many other countries in Asia as well as around the United States. I started building my international network in earnest. I was welcomed, invited, included, respected, and for the very first time in my life, I felt seen, complete, and whole.

Time flies when you're having fun and soon my time in the Air Force was coming to an end. Sure, I could have stayed in, but my thought process was...

1. I really love this but I'm quickly gaining a lot more responsibility, which is making me love it less. If I leave now, I will always have good things to say about the experience.
2. I feel confident in my ability to navigate my way in the world without the military. I would like the freedom to set out as I please.

FIRST STOP, NICARAGUA

People always ask why of all places, I chose to make Granada, Nicaragua, my home after the Air Force. It's simple, really. I had heard good things about the country. Warm weather, friendly people, beautiful girls, low cost of living. My plan was to go there, open a bar with the money I had saved, and launch a whole new chapter of my life.

I arrived and immediately fell in love with a strikingly beautiful girl, and all my plans changed.

I stayed with a family to learn the lay of the land and their customs. I signed up for Spanish classes and volunteered to help the English teachers there. This gave me a really good start on meeting new people and building my network. I often had dinner in small hotels where tourist backpackers stayed, so I could meet people from around the world. Three times per week I would do "take a stranger to lunch" day, where I would pick someone local who was at their work or maybe even walking down the street and offer to take them to lunch. It was always interesting to see who I would meet.

As they do, however, my romantic relationship had demands.

My original plan to open the bar wasn't going to cut it anymore. I needed something better because I was planning to settle down and have a family.

HOME AGAIN

The most lucrative offer I got was to return to the States for a job in the oil and gas industry. I came back to make that happen, but there were hiccups in the process. The job didn't start when it was supposed to, so I had to seek other employment in the interim.

A friend who was an armed security guard suggested I come work with him, and I did. The job didn't pay well, so I decided to supplement that income with commodity futures trading. I was determined to avoid the mistakes that bankrupted me in my youth and do it right this time.

Here's to falling back on old habits.

As you already can imagine, luck did not shine down on me. I proceeded to lose all of my money. Then my girl down in Nicaragua broke up with me.

And there I was.

The combination of all of those things together knocked me flat on my face. It felt like the flame went out inside me and I went cold. I withdrew into myself to attempt to find comfort in isolation.

I was supposed to be free in the world, laughing in the wind, and yet somehow, I had managed to lose everything, including myself. Nobody respects security guards. Every day I had to go into work and get shit on by people. I looked into going back into the Air Force, but that wasn't an option. I felt trapped, cornered, weak.

How did I get here? Once again, mocked, ignored, invisible. A friend told me I was depressed. *Depressed? Really? You think?* I didn't know. All I knew was something wasn't right with me. I was off.

I was so tired. So. Tired. But it wasn't anything that sleep could fix.

So, one evening I came up with a solution.

Being an armed security guard, you always have options. My option this particular evening was to have a nice dinner, make my rounds, then in the wee small hours of the morning, blow my brains out.

Dinner was good: spicy chicken strips with honey mustard, mashed potatoes, and a slice of apple pie.

I made my rounds, smiled, shook some hands, and honestly felt better than I'd felt in ages simply because I knew this was my last night.

At about 2 a.m., I pulled my patrol car into an alley (a clean alley—I'm not a savage), put the car in park, unholstered my pistol, slowly pulled back the hammer, and gently placed the pistol into my mouth.

Interesting how clear your thinking gets when you have the taste of gunmetal on your tongue and cold steel grinding against your teeth.

My life wasn't supposed to be like this; it was supposed to be different...better.

My finger caressed the trigger, like the inside of a woman's thigh. A single tear welled up in my right eye and rolled down my cheek. I watched as it fell, seemingly in slow motion, and landed on my pants, absorbing in.

Soon I would be the same as the tear. Forgotten. Nothing more than a memory.

I closed my eyes, held my breath, and...

Somewhere in my head a voice spoke to me. But it wasn't my voice. At least it didn't sound like mine. It was confident. Assured. Empowered.

It said, "You have to save your own life."

What? I was going nuts and had to hurry this thing up.

I heard it again. "You have to save your own life."

"But how?" I asked.

Silence…

I knew I had to listen. Disobedience was not an option. I carefully removed my finger from the trigger, slowly pulled the gun out of my mouth, and exhaled deeply.

For a long moment I looked into the distance, sitting still, staring at nothing.

Then, after a quiet eternity, I blinked my eyes and whispered, "All right, fine." I holstered my pistol, put the car in gear, and pulled out of the alley to continue my patrols.

Since no one was coming to save me, it was up to me. I decided to imagine a better future for myself, despite everything in my life pointing in the other direction.

How do I move forward? I'll do whatever it takes, but I need to know what the next step is. What's the "trick?" What's the "secret?" What am I missing?

BREAKTHROUGH

I was watching videos one evening and heard a saying for

what must have been the millionth time. This time it had special significance. "Your Network is your Net-Worth." If you can level up your network, you'll level up your life.

A light bulb flashed in my head. *Wait a minute. If that's the case, then I am far wealthier than I think.* I knew a lot of people and, more importantly, was known by a lot of people. Plus, I had the skills to meet new people and navigate social situations like a boss!

I know I'm making it sound simple, and it is simple, but it definitely isn't easy.

I'm sure you have heard the saying, "You are the result of the five people you spend the most time around." I realized the five people I spent the most time around weren't living the type of life I wanted to live and couldn't teach me what I needed to know.

I needed to level up.

I had to surround myself with people who achieved more than I did, people I could trust and respect, who thought big, had accomplished big things, and use them as a guide to help me get to where I wanted to go.

I looked for different types of meetup groups. I attended many, made a lot of new friends, and built a lot of new professional and personal relationships. I secured the job in oil and gas, which opened a lot more doors. I got on high-end lists, which got me invited to exclusive events. I found good mentors and volunteered my time, doing some work for free. Sometimes I had to pay to be in the room, but I was in the right rooms and that was a good start.

I showed up, watched, listened, and studied. My life began to turn around. Before long, I was making significant progress.

As I was able to travel more and get invited to high-end, exclusive events, friends and associates asked me to show them how to do the same. It started informally: tips here, coaching and guidance there. As demand grew, I decided to streamline the process and put together an actual blueprint.

WHERE AM I NOW?

I have a strong international network of friends, associates, and colleagues that I add value to. By doing so, I live the life I always wanted and dreamed about. I love travel and have visited friends in thirty-seven countries so far. I've had the pleasure of attending some very exclusive events in some of those countries.

I love sailboats, airplanes, and the occasional polo match. And now, I often get invited to go sailing, go deep sea fishing, ride in private airplanes, and attend polo matches. It's awesome!

I love the experiences, and even more than that, I enjoy the company of good friends during my travels. I don't own a lot of material stuff because I'm a bit of a minimalist, but when I do interesting things and host events, I invite my friends. If I charter a yacht, I'm not going yachting alone. I have to invite someone to share the experience, right? Why not you?

So anyway, I started showing introverted, shy, and socially awkward people how to network better so they can be calm, confident, and approachable in social settings. It was a big hurdle for me in my life, so I really enjoy helping others gain the skill to do it. It's simple once you know what to do. So, I teach exactly what to do.

I understand that not everyone wants to build a worldwide network. Some just want to be able to navigate their office holiday party better or socialize with the other parents at their child's Little League game. I cover that, too. I share techniques that make sense and are intuitive, so it's not like you have to memorize stuff.

Once I built out my network, I felt like I finally had food in my belly, and that felt good.

Now I'm opening the kitchen to you, and "Everybody eats when they come to MY house!"

So, let's do this, shall we?

No more strangers having forgettable exchanges.

Step out of the shadows and into the light.

Let's go!

A NOTE FROM ME TO YOU

Hey, just a quick note from me to you. This book is about high-level networking, so it's about navigating social situations but also leveling up—because for me I wanted to not only be more comfortable speaking with people but also surround myself with high achievers. And so, it's not just about going to fancy events and sticking your pinky out while drinking your tea or watching polo and riding in a helicopter. It's ultimately about people, the relationships you build and the friendships that are made.

The reason I want to surround myself with high achievers is because they say you become who you surround yourself with. I knew it would make me develop better habits and I'd have access to a lot more opportunities if I was around people who were doing a lot of cool things.

So, building relationships with people who are really pushing the limits of their comfort zones and getting things done. That's the path I chose.

This isn't theory; this is what I do, day in and day out. I'm in the trenches actually doing the things I teach you in this book, so it's real and I'm not holding anything back. I am presenting to you everything I've learned.

I hope this book serves you well on the path YOU choose. I'm not telling you to blindly accept everything I say. I just invite you try it out and see what works for you.

Have an open mind, step up, show up, and I think you will be very pleasantly surprised at the results you get.

Chapter Two

SET UP FOR SUCCESS

BARRIER IDENTIFICATION

We have to figure out what's holding you back, what has kept you from doing this before.

So, let's identify some barriers.

Was it *time*? Maybe you're just like, "Well, I don't have enough time to go out and socialize and network. I'd like to do it, but I don't have the time."

(You can still do it with very little time.)

Money. "Well, Nick, I'd like to go out to high-end events and meet people. I'd also like to attend regular events, too, but you know it costs money."

(It doesn't always cost money.)

Comfort zone. Getting out of your comfort zone is probably a barrier for all of us.

I know it has been a big thing for me, and I'm sure it's most likely a challenge for you as well. I'm going to show you how to expand your comfort zone.

Figure out what your major barriers are and write them down somewhere.

What's been holding you back?

What is the most likely barrier you will face when trying to actually move forward to put your new networking life into action? I'm sure you have an idea of what it might be by looking at your past behaviors and/or habits.

It's really helpful to know what's been holding you back, so write it down and think about it. Think about what has kept you from being able to network at the level you want to.

It is great to be knowledgeable of where you have gotten stuck before and what might be an obstacle now, because as we come across those, you'll see where you got hung up and how you can pass through it. But you need to know where your sticking points are.

Figure it out, write it down, do it now—and then we'll move on.

FIND YOUR PREFERRED LEVEL OF NETWORKING

I mentioned earlier that this book is about high-level networking, how to get to know the who's who, the upper-level folk. But at the same time, that might not be where you want to be. You might not want to meet those people. I've spent time in all the areas at all levels. Some interests in some groups appeal to me and some don't. I personally enjoy the variety. I am comfortable with that, but you might want something different.

People are people with a lot of the same issues and concerns. So maybe you just want to do workplace or industry networking. Perhaps your goal is local networking in just your city or state. You have to think about your personal goal and vision. Where do you want to be?

How can this information serve you best to get to where you want to be? Maybe you don't want to go yachting and on helicopter rides. I don't know. I'm just showing you what's worked for me and my students. You can use all of these skills and techniques to be able to move forward, level up, and expand your relationships and network. I personally like the idea of having friends around the world, and I do my best to provide a lot of value to them and they do the same for me.

These principles and techniques will help you make your network as big as you want it to be. But you need to decide what level you want to play at and adjust to your specific circumstances.

SHOW UP

All right. One more quick and very important point and then we're going to get started. The most important thing: show up. You have to show up and put in the work. If you don't show up, then nothing is going to happen. So, first and foremost, you're going to have to show up *every time* especially in the early parts of trying to get your networking to the level you want it to be.

Show up and follow the steps. You will know what to do. You're going to see great progress. But once again, I cannot emphasize it enough.

Show the hell up.

When you're invited, show up. If you haven't been invited but you find an event, show up. Always show up. You must show up.

So, now that I have said "show up" way too many times, what are you going to do?

Show the f*** up!

FIND AN EVENT

First and foremost, for you to be the networking king or queen, you're going to have to actually go someplace where you can network, an event of some sort. Yes, with people.

Now, it might be a work event, a birthday party, a wine tasting, or it could be something that one of your friends or even you are putting together; it doesn't matter, but you need an event.

If you don't already have one in mind, you can always look online. If you have an interest of some sort, you can just type it in to the internet and look for events.

So, say, for example, glassblowing. You're like, "Yeah, I'm curious about a glassblower's meetup somewhere." You can find it!

There's a website called Meetup. You type in glassblowing meetup, and *boom*, there it is! You'll see when and where the glassblowers get together to hang out and talk about stuff.

If that's not your thing, type in something else like "bee-keeping meetup," because you could say, "Well you know

I'm curious about beekeepers and what they do. so I'll just go. I'll just go sit in, and I'll meet some people there."

Whatever it is that you have an interest in, type it in, whether it's "stamp collecting meetup" or "people who like *Battlestar Galactica* meetup." It could be anything, and usually there's a group of people who are getting together to meet and talk about that. So, get online and do your thing. Find a meetup of something you're curious about. Remember there really is no limit. For example, I've gone to meetups for private pilots. I'm not a pilot, but I thought it would be interesting to meet some private pilots and see what they're up to. So, I went. Or "fine art appreciation meetup"—I wondered what that was about so...yep, count me in!

So keep in mind, it doesn't have to be something you are passionate about. You can merely be curious and decide you are interested in meeting the type of people who would attend something like that.

Another place to look for events is the newspaper. Believe it or not, people still look at the newspaper, and there is information on events in there. You might see some cool event that's coming to your city. It could be anything, such as going to the symphony or something like a beer or wine tasting. There are lots of things that are happening in your city, your town, and your country.

If you are so inclined, there are also international events you can go to. However, I recommend starting off someplace local so it's easier for you to start putting your feelers out and start building up your skills.

Of all the different options when you're starting, it's easy to start locally. However, sometimes for your job, you might be sent to some other city for a conference or something like that, which is great! I personally love traveling to attend different events, but it's up to you, your level, and your goals.

It's up to you what level you want to be and where you want to network. I like a variety of atmospheres, so I'll go to some very fancy high-end events, and then I'll do some regular events as well because I enjoy a full range. But for you, maybe you're really trying to focus on getting into some high-end events, and that's cool. Or maybe you're just trying to learn the basics and simply handle day-to-day social situations or elevate your position at work or in your industry.

For now, I want you to find some event that you're going to attend to start practicing this stuff. So, get online and look around, or if you already know an event you want to attend, write down what your event is. Do it now.

Put it on the calendar and then as you work through these steps, you will know what to pay attention to that will serve you most for that particular circumstance, and you'll have a deadline to keep you motivated.

HIGH-END LISTS

High-end lists have served me very well and will do the same for you, so you want to pay attention if you have any interest in being invited to high-end events.

So, you say, "Nick, I know you said that I'd be getting invited to stuff. How do I do that? How do I get invited to special events at luxury car dealerships where they tell you about the cars and then beg you to drive them? How do I get invited to the polo championships or a private museum event and other high-end cool stuff?"

Well, you probably haven't ever thought of this before but what you want to do is spam yourself.

What do I mean by that? Well, there's a list for everything, and you need to be on the list.

Earlier we talked about finding an event.

So, find your event, but in the meanwhile you're going to need to plant seeds, so later on it'll pay off in invitations for you.

Make a list of different high-end things or brands. Then

you are going to go online and type those events or brand names in. So, for example, Ritz Carlton. You'll type in Ritz Carlton, and on their site, there will be a place to join a list. Join that list, add your name, email, and if there is a place for your mailing address, add that too. Then move on to the next site—for example, Maserati.com—and add your name and email to their list.

And then if you like, type in "private jet charter," go down the list of sites, and put your email in, put your address in. Jet charters, helicopter charters, yacht charters, high-end real estate—put your name, put your address. Jewelry, like Tiffany's, Cartier, Rolex—go add your email address and your mailing address.

Keep going with anything like this—I saw caviar the other day. What did I do? I was like, "Oh, there is a caviar event!" (I'll have a story about caviar later.) I put my email address in there. So, my advice to you is this: for any sort of high-end event, high-end fundraisers, or estate sales (and things like that), put in your email address or your mailing address, always!

So, now you are on a list. You are on a list as someone who's interested in luxury items and experiences. And the list owner usually sells your name to other lists, so then you get in the system as being someone who likes luxury events and luxury items. And yes, you will get a bunch of emails, and yes, you will get a bunch of actual mail in your mailbox from these places. This is how it starts, and it doesn't happen overnight, but over a period of a few months someone is going to send you an invitation to some sort of event. It might be something like a private event held by a jeweler where they're going to show you special pieces of jewelry.

It might be a luxury car dealership.

When Maserati came out with their SUV, they sent out some invites saying, "Hey, come down to the Maserati dealership. We're going to tell you about this SUV we're releasing." And then you show up, have some finger sandwiches, and they tell you all about it and give you the brochures and all that. Then when the vehicle is actually released, they pretty much beg you to come drive it. And you'll say, "No, I don't want to drive it." And then they will say, "Drive it. Just take it for a spin, take it out for the evening, show your friends." And there you are!

But here's the thing, when you get an invite, the first invite you get, you HAVE to go. This goes back to what I said about showing up. You must show up, and you have to do it the first time. If you don't show up, then all your effort is going to be wasted.

Once you actually show up, there's a whole other list—a list of people who show up to events for high-end things.

So, you will not only be on the list of people who are interested in high-end things, but you'll be on a list of people who show up to high-end things. So, that's a whole other list. And, once you have been invited and you show up, you will start getting other invitations to things as well, other luxury events.

Then if you happen to buy something while you are at one of these events, that's another list. That is a list of people who BUY luxury things, and that is the best list to be on.

Now, naturally that takes some money, and you don't necessarily have to buy a luxury car or a jet or something like that. You just have to make some kind of purchase—for example, if there's a fundraiser, you can donate a token amount, or if there's an auction for something small, you can get that. Or, if you charter a yacht for a half day or something like that, you will also qualify. You'll be on a list of people who bought, and that is the best list because those people get invited to more things than anyone else because they are proven buyers of high-end things.

The goal is to eventually get on one of those lists. But it starts off by being on just the "I'm interested in luxury items" list. Find as many lists as you can; put in your name, email, and your mailing address.

This technique has a snowball effect. You start off by spamming yourself, getting yourself on as many lists of luxury items, high-end items, and events, whatever you can think of. If there's some kind of opera or symphony in town, put your name on the list. You don't have to go unless you get an invite—then you have to go. But just get your name on a list. That's a great starting point.

In the meanwhile, you're picking out some other place to go. You're picking out your basic event that you're going to attend. But you're planting seeds for later by getting yourself spammed by luxury, high-end places. Get your name on the list. Stop what you're doing now. Pause. Do it right now. Take action. Get your name on some list right now. Don't even start the next chapter until you have put your name on at least ten lists if you're interested in high-end networking. Do it just to get the ball rolling. And every day be on the lookout. If you see a new list, put your name on that too. Do it.

You may not be able to afford high-end items or events at the moment, but once again, this is about laying the foundation and getting known in these circles. You may not need money to participate in some of these experiences or outings, and being "in the room" at events like these may lead to opportunities and relationships that end up with you making more money.

THE BUYER'S LIST

All right, hopefully you have put your name on at least ten high-end, luxury item lists to get the ball rolling. Later on, you can—if you have the money—really elevate your invite potential by moving yourself to a buyer's list.

And so, what worked for me was chartering a helicopter. I was staying at a hotel, noticed they had a helicopter pad, and thought, *Oh, I think I'll take a helicopter*. So, I went to the front desk and said, "Hey, I need a helicopter."

And they said, "Okay." And they made a phone call and told me, "It's $600 an hour, how many hours do you require?"

And I said, "One hour, please."

Because is it ever going to get any cheaper? Probably not, and I wanted to do it. I wanted to take a helicopter ride. So, the helicopter came, I grabbed my cousin, and we went on a one-hour helicopter ride. I told the pilot, "Fly around. Show us some stuff for an hour and then take us back." And I was then on a list of people who charter helicopters.

Shortly after that, I chartered a yacht for four hours. I wanted to do it because, you know, hey, let's see how much fun we can have. So, I did it, and it wasn't too expensive, I suppose. Now, there are a lot of yachts that the minimum time to charter is a few days. A lot of people won't do four hours, but you'll be able to find someone who will let you do it. And four hours is plenty. You go out, have a good time, and come back. But now, you're on a list of people who charter yachts, and that's a pretty good place to be.

That puts you in a whole other category. But remember you start off just being a person who's interested. Get on those lists and then the lists all intertwine and compile. If you can get on the list of interest, then on a list of people who show up when they're invited, and then on a list of people who buy, you'll be in the ultimate sweet spot. Now it might be a little too much right out of the gate, but I'm just telling you that this is where you want to progress to. Some people could probably do it right away, but for others it might take a little time. Maybe it's not in your budget to do something like that—I understand. But these are the steps to get on all the best lists. Start off just by getting your name on as many "simply interested in luxury items" lists as you can.

GET PRE-KNOWN

Okay. Before you actually go to your events, one super, super valuable thing that will really pay off for you, if you can do it (you can't always do it, but if you can), is to be pre-known. How do you get pre-known? There are usually two ways.

Online...a lot of times these days people will have a Facebook group, a WhatsApp group, a Telegram group, or some other kind of online group that is for people who are attending the event to socialize a little bit before the event starts.

It could be weeks or a few months before the actual event. So, what you want to do is get on there and be active, not super over the top, but active and involved.

Join the online group and observe. You'll see who the main people are in that group, and then you want to piggyback on them, comment on some of their comments, and comment on some of their posts.

Then when other people are interacting, interact with them and don't take some crazy, super controversial stances or anything; just chill out, and if you see something you like, compliment it. Compliment or thank them for sharing certain things, or ask them a question and then get a little conversation going if you can. There's always going to be a question you can ask or something you can compliment them on, and just follow generally those who seem to be the main players in this online group.

Be active enough so they get familiar with you like, "Oh, this is Steven. Steven has been interacting with me for three weeks now. We've discussed X, Y, and Z."

As you get closer to the event, you'll say, "Hey, I look forward to seeing you/meeting up with you at the event." That will give you a little advantage when you arrive at the event.

Another way is that sometimes the night before an event, someone will say, "Hey, we're all..." or "I am..." or "A group of us are meeting at this bar for drinks," or, "We're going to go have appetizers here."

Or, sometimes they'll say, "Hey, I..." and it'll just be one person. "Hey, I'm flying in tonight at 8:00 p.m. I'm going to be at this bar if anyone wants to join me to have a beer." Or, they might say, "Hey, I'm coming into the airport at this time; if anyone wants to share a taxi or something, let me know." So, if this happens, this is something you may want to show up to.

This has happened to me many times where I'll be tired and just want to sleep, but then somebody will say, "Hey, I'm going to be at this bar having a beer if anyone wants to go."

And my response is, "Yes, I'll meet you. I'll be right there."

And then, I will show up against my natural will, and it might be that one person or there might be three or four. It's usually not some massive group, but there might be four of us who show up. Everybody has come on equal footing because it's not like, "Oh, it's a gang of us who know each other and you're the outsider." Usually, it's just a group of people who don't know each other yet.

And so, it's not a really uncomfortable thing. You have this opportunity to go in on a much smaller scale than the event is going to be and maybe have a beer or a cocktail or just some French fries with one, two, three, four people in a different setting like a bar, pub, restaurant, or something like that, where you can actually sit across from them, get to know them, have a laugh, and exchange ideas before the event.

And in that way when you arrive at the actual event, you're pre-known. You already have this little group that you're familiar with, so when you show up, you'll say, "Hey, there's Phil, Jim, and Sarah..."

People will recognize you, and you will recognize them, and that makes a huge difference when you walk in.

So, if you can be pre-known, this is a really great way to do it. Either do one or both of these things if you can. Be active on those chat groups for the event beforehand. Or, when somebody says, "Hey, I'm going out..." join them; or, you can do it too. Say, "Hey, I'm going to this bar for a beer, if anybody wants to join me."

You can be the one who kicks it off; if no one else is doing it, you can do it. You can do it yourself so then you can control the atmosphere. If there's a certain restaurant you feel comfortable in or a certain place, you can say, "I'm going

to be here. Meet me here, anyone who wants to show up."
And somebody will show up.

If you do both, that's even better. If you can be active in
the group and you can also meet with one person or a few
people beforehand, you will be golden. This has served me
really well. I made some really great connections by meeting people before an event even starts.

Something to think about: when you find your event like
your assignment was earlier, put it on the calendar and then
look to see if there is some online chat group that you can
join as well. If it's a big-enough event, usually they'll have
some kind of a chat group that goes along with it. If you
can find the chat group, join it. And if you can do any sort
of pre-event stuff, even better.

Put that into action. Write it down. Get to work. Put in the
work. Show up. Do it.

TIME MANAGEMENT

I'd like to address time management because people often
ask me where I find the time to network. I understand it
can be difficult to find the time between work and family
obligations to attend events.

I suggest you simply do more connecting and networking

during things you are already doing and/or making more time. I'll explain what I mean.

Connecting better at things you're already doing. If you are spending a lot of time taking your kids to their events, use that time to practice connecting with the other parents at those events. If you are working long hours at your occupation, practice your networking skills with those you come in contact with there. I understand it can be difficult depending on the type of job you have. For example, if you are an underwater welder, how much interaction with other people are you going to be able to have? So...yes, I understand it depends. When I was working long hours in a laboratory, I was around the same people all day long, but I would make it a point to visit other sections of the company outside of the laboratory and "make the rounds." It was refreshing to get out, get some air, and also get in some practice with my social skills.

When I talk about making more time, what I mean is that you can reduce the time you spend doing things that aren't adding value to your life. You can watch less TV. You can sleep a little less. You can free up all sorts of time by reducing your internet usage.

Probably the best way to free up time is to simply organize your days better. If you organize your days and weeks better, you will free up a lot more time than you think, to take on whatever project you like including building your network.

A friend of mine, Craig Ballantyne, wrote the books *The Perfect Day Formula* and *The Perfect Week Formula*. Both of these are amazing in their ability to clearly break down the steps in how to organize and prioritize your time. Check those books out if you want to organize your time better.

My point is, we all have twenty-four hours in a day, and if we make better use of our time, we can get where we want to go and accomplish our goals.

Let me also touch on a common question. "If I'm meeting so many new people, how am I supposed to keep up with all of them and maintain all of the relationships?"

As new people come into your network, you will naturally rank them, and some people will require more time and others less time. You'll meet a lot of new people, but often you will not come away with the one SOLID one. So, it doesn't build up as fast as you'd think. Also, with some people, as you spend time and get to know them better, you discover you don't really want to prioritize them, or you may even learn that you don't really like them so you may choose to let them fade.

You prune a tree so it can grow and come back stronger. The same applies to your network. I've been known to do an occasional purge if I felt it was necessary, and oftentimes it has made my network stronger.

STAY AT THE MOST EXPENSIVE HOTEL YOU CAN AFFORD

Here is a tip from one of my mentors that I got a lot of value out of and would like to share with you. When you travel, try to stay at the most expensive hotel you can afford. You can get the cheapest room there if you like, but it is good to be at the best hotel you can afford. The reason is because of the people you are likely to meet there.

While you are having a cocktail at the bar, or hitting the treadmill at the gym in the morning, or relaxing by the pool, you will be exposed to the other people staying at the hotel.

There will be opportunities to kick off conversations. Usually people staying at high-level hotels are action takers who are efficient at getting things done. You may meet someone who can really move the needle on your project or know someone who can, or you simply might make a great new friend.

It's a good habit to adapt, plus, you get to stay in really nice hotels. That's a great perk, too!

SUMMARY

So, to summarize what we've covered so far, I want you to identify barriers.

What's been holding you back? What's been stopping you in the past? And what do you think might pop up and become a problem as you start moving forward?

You have to identify that and know what it is so you can get out in front of it. If you do that, it'll be easier to address and move past it.

You need to find an event. Then, put it on the calendar. Make a plan to go because you have to show up and put in the work. Find something you are interested in attending and get it on the calendar so there's a deadline, a date you need to be ready by, and it will help you learn faster.

Spam yourself. While you're waiting for the event to come around, you want to get your name on as many lists as possible. If you are interested in high-level networking and getting invited to exclusive, high-end events one day, you're going to have to start building that foundation, and the foundation is getting your name on as many high-end, luxury lists as possible.

You have to actually put in the work by thinking of different things like caviar, jewelry, yacht charters, helicopter charters, fine art exhibits, all kinds of different events and different activities that are high-end. Put your name on the list.

It's really cool when you get stuff in the mail to look through and say, "Oh, look at this. Look at what's available. Look what somebody is doing."

Put your name on the list to get the momentum going, then get your mindset right.

Getting pre-known: this is HUGE, and you won't always have an opportunity to do it. But if you can do it, do it because it absolutely makes a big difference.

Get on those event message boards and start establishing some relationships. Don't get too wild and crazy with it. Keep it light and simple. But make yourself known on there.

And if somebody wants to meet up sometime before an event, you go. You show up and you're there. You can also be the one who extends the invite to other people. Do your best to try to get that pre-known status. It'll really help out.

Manage your time properly and everything will fall into place. We all have twenty-four hours in a day; you want to make the most of it because it's your most valuable asset.

Remember to stay at the most expensive hotel you can afford. You'll be exposed to people who are movers and shakers. People who get things done.

Next, we're going to talk about what happens when you actually go to the event, and it's going to be awesome!

Chapter Three

MAKING CONNECTIONS

Now for the good stuff, making connections. You have picked out an event, and you have it on the calendar. You are ready to go connect with people, make new friends, reconnect with old friends, and establish relationships.

We're going to go through exactly what to do when you show up. It's going to be exciting!

And it's going to be good! This is what you're here for, the actual networking stuff. Let's get into it!

EXPECTATIONS

So, what should you expect when you go in?

You're not going to just go in there and take over the world.

A really good expectation is to try to walk out with *one* solid connection. One person you would like to see again, about whom you would say, "This seems like someone I would like to be friends with, follow up with, get to know, and spend time with."

Your goal is to try to find ONE.

You might find more than that, or you might not, but you are trying to make at least one solid connection you want to follow up with that you find fascinating or interesting.

You wouldn't think it should be that hard, right? Sometimes things just don't click, but sometimes they do, and you will get more than one—you'll get several!

But you need to manage your expectations; you're going for one. If it doesn't happen, no big deal; that's normal too. You're still good, you're learning. And if you get more, awesome!

So, set expectations at one solid connection. Cool, what's next?

HOW TO DRESS

You are going to want to figure out what the standard is. You're NOT trying to blend in. I repeat...DON'T BLEND IN!

You're trying to stand out, but you don't want to stand out *too* much. You're not there to be a peacock with your feathers all on display. You want to find out what the standard attire is and go just a little bit higher, or dress the standard and add an accessory that will be memorable.

Maybe you have a belt or something that is unusual. Maybe, if you're a man, you have a pocket square that's a little different. Or, your shoes: men or women can wear shoes that are a little brighter or have something different about them. You should have some kind of accessory that is noteworthy. If you're going to go standard like everybody else, you need one accessory that is unique; or dress a little bit better than the standard AND add an accessory.

Don't underdress. You're not *that* cool. We're trying to make you remembered and memorable in the most positive way.

Think about people you have met in the past who had something that stood out about them with their clothing. I remember at an event I met a guy who wore a tucked-in Hawaiian shirt and had his hair parted down the middle. I was thinking, *What's up with this guy?* but if I live to be a thousand years old, I'll still remember him. I'm not saying you should go to that extreme; I'm just saying I'm sure everyone at that event remembers that guy.

ALONE OR PLUS-ONE

When attending events, is it better to show up alone or with a partner? Let's explore these options, each having positives and negatives. Most of the time for me, I'm alone, but sometimes I'll bring a date or a friend.

Usually I prefer to go alone because you can do certain things when you're alone that you can't do if you're with a partner, and I feel I usually end up meeting a lot more people if I'm alone. However, there are also certain things you can accomplish with a partner you can't do if you're alone. For me, I have a very strange schedule and many of my events are out of town or on short notice, so at times it can be difficult to get somebody else to go. A lot of these techniques I'm going to tell you about will be from the perspective that you're going by yourself, or at least arriving by yourself. But I'll also give you the angle for if you have somebody with you.

If you have the option to bring somebody with you, it's easier. But, most of the time in my experience, I show up alone and it works out really well.

SHOW UP EARLY

You don't want to be one of these people who shows up—what do they call it?—casually late, fashionably late, or something, where you make an appearance: "Hey, everybody, I'm here. I've arrived!"

And you don't want to show up on time. You want to show up early. Why?

The reason is that you get the lay of the land; you can get there, see what's going on, see how it's set up, and then you can position yourself for the best advantage.

If you show up late, or on time, everyone is already settled or getting settled in, people are in their groups, and you have to come in and try to do your thing. You'll still be able to do it, but it's way better if you're one of the early people so you can decide, *What part of the room do I want to be in?*

You'll be able to position yourself to your best advantage. Then as people arrive and come in, you're already established. It'll be much easier for you to engage from an established position versus just popping in late and trying to navigate your way through it.

If you are an extrovert, maybe you show up late because you're cool like that. But for introverts, I'm telling you this way is better. Show up early and you will be able to navigate the scene, get established, and get comfortable. Be early.

YOUR PHONE

You showed up early. You're out in the parking lot or outside of the building. Take this time to get centered. Get your mind right; remember why you're here. You're trying to make one connection. Take a few deep breaths and put your phone on silent. You're not going to mess with your phone. I'll say it again: you're not going to mess with your phone. Don't mess with your phone.

So, what are you going to do?

If you've retained *anything*, you would have said, "Show up!" But I'll take "Don't mess with your phone," too.

These days most people will go into an event with the intent of being social and then stand around messing with their phones. You're not there to be messing with your phone, and it makes you less approachable. Don't mess with your phone. Put it on silent. Don't bring that phone out. Don't bring it out. Do NOT bring your phone out during the thing. Now, if you need to do something with your phone, then check your text messages and all that—or look at what the Kardashians are doing—when you go to the bathroom or something. But do not mess with your phone while you are in an event.

You can leave it in the car. You can put it in your pocket or purse. Don't bring that sucker out. Don't bring it out unless someone is giving you their phone number or something like that, and only then can you bring it out and put the phone number in. But don't be messing with your phone.

It is not going to help you. It's going to work against you in so many ways.

So, breathe and focus on meeting one person and making a connection. You're going to meet a lot of people, but you're trying to make one solid connection. You're not going to mess with the phone—you're not going to mess with your phone. All right? Don't mess with the phone!

ENTERING THE EVENT

When you enter the event, you're going to want to do it a certain way. You want your energy level to be a little bit higher than the room. It should be like you're excited to be there. Or like something exciting and awesome just happened to you right before you walked in the door. You want to be like, "Yeah, this is awesome! I've been waiting for this!"

One thing I try to do if I have the time and the resources is watch or listen to a clip of stand-up comedy before I enter a social scene. The reason is, if I can get in a good laugh beforehand, it really loosens things up and gets me in the right frame of mind. If I can't do that, then I just proceed anyway.

The best way to walk in, and this applies to men and women (I heard this tip from fellow social strategist, Tripp Kramer), is to walk like you're wearing a cape. And I really liked that. So, I'm going to say it too. Walk like you're wearing a cape and you want your cape to flow properly. So, you're going to walk with confidence and smoothness. You want your imaginary cape to have a nice drape and a nice flow to it. So, in my head, as I enter, I'll say to myself, "Cape Walk!"

Those of you who spend a lot of time around me might say, "Hmmm, that's odd; usually you walk like a small woodland creature on the lookout for predators."

Sure, that's fair; it's my default walk, usually when I'm cold and I don't think anyone is looking. But, for social events... Cape Walk!

You're not always going to remember all of these things, but when you do remember, kick it in! The Cape Walk strategy will give you the proper walk. Women usually walk really nicely already so this is mostly for guys, but women should try it too because it gives you an extra touch of elegance and grace. So, the point is if you do the Cape Walk, it's going to serve you well.

Your posture will be on point, and you'll look confident.

IMPOSTER SYNDROME

Let's talk about imposter syndrome. This is when you feel like you don't quite belong.

This can work both ways. You might be in a private suite at the Kentucky Derby thinking, *Hmmm, I'm not sure if I really belong here; what am I supposed to do?* Or you might be in a village in a third-world country in a small shack made of sticks and mud watching your host prepare dinner over an open fire and once again think, *Hmmm, I'm not sure if I really belong here; what am I supposed to do?*

Settle in, be yourself, observe, and go with the flow. That's really all there is to it. As I mentioned earlier, don't try to be what you're not. So at the Kentucky Derby event, if you don't know what to do, don't try to pretend like you know what to do. The easiest thing is to ask your host or someone close by, "How does this work? It's my first time."

Same with the village: "Can I help in any way? Can you explain the custom?"

Recently I took a trip to Sri Lanka to visit a friend of mine who invited me. He is an attorney there. One evening he invited me to attend a cocktail party for high-end criminal defense attorneys. Now as you may know, I am not an attorney and I knew it would be out of my comfort zone, but I agreed to go. It was a good time.

What did I do? I didn't pretend to be some kind of big shot. I was just an ordinary guy. I simply enjoyed the food and a cocktail and practiced my observation skills. The conversations were mostly about things that I have no idea about, so I didn't engage in those. When the conversation turned to world events, I contributed when and where I could. I made a few new friends and consider the evening a success.

I think the most important thing to remember is mindset. If I walk into the village scenario, I'm not there to judge or think I'm better than anyone. I'm there to observe and learn. I'll ask questions and figure it out as I go.

With the high-end settings, the same occurs. I don't go in feeling inferior to anyone, because I'm there, I'm on the list, I've been invited just like everyone else attending. I don't overstate my position in life and try to make myself important. I keep it understated and observe, ask questions, and go with the flow.

I keep in mind that a lot of the big shots and VIPs don't really know what to do either. I know this because I know quite a few VIPs, and when I speak to them about events, they feel the same way as the rest of us. They're trying to figure it out too and battle with the same imposter demons.

One good tip I heard recently from Susie Moore, who is a life coach and advice columnist, is when you start to feel that imposter syndrome creeping in, say to yourself, *It's OK, I'm becoming X.* So, for example, if you are at a polo event it can be, *It's OK, I'm becoming a polo enthusiast.*

The point is, remember you are there at the event, and that's what matters. Whether you are having a meal with the janitor or with the governor, don't focus on yourself. Focus on them, observe, listen, ask questions. You'll be all right.

If all else fails and you need a backup plan, use the dream technique.

Tell yourself, "This isn't really happening. This is a dream, and you can do anything in your dreams!"

DUKE COOKIE FACE

This is one of my favorite tips. If you don't remember anything else from this book, remember this one tip and it will provide you with tremendous value each and every time you use it. This alone is worth the price of admission!

This tip is mainly for when you are seated somewhere. I love this move because it works so amazingly well. I call it "Duke Cookie Face."

"Duke Cookie Face" is a way to sit. Here is the story behind it. I was at a corporate holiday party of a woman I was dating at the time. I didn't know anyone, and I wanted to make sure I made a good impression with my girlfriend's coworkers.

One thing I was aware of: you never know who is looking at you, sizing you up.

I knew her coworkers were going to be curious about me, and I would only have a chance to meet a few of them. The rest would just observe me from a distance and draw their conclusions. What could I do to have the maximum positive effect?

I figured if I could make sure my body language was correct, everything else would fall into place. So, I imagined a duke, a nobleman, and I thought, *How would a nobleman sit?* You're not the king, so you don't have the stress and worries of running stuff, but you're pretty high up there, right? And so, you sit up like you're *somebody*. Good posture, back straight but not stiff, in a sort of relaxed position.

So how you picture a duke or duchess sitting, that's how you sit. Open body language, you're confident, maybe even lean on something casually. And that's the duke or duchess part of the method.

Then your face. Your facial expression should be like if you arrive at your best friend's house, walk in the door, and are hit with the smell of fresh-baked cookies. You love cookies, and you know they're going to offer you some.

Cookies are imminent. Cookies are coming. You're getting a cookie soon!

So, your facial expression is saying, "Cookies are coming. Cookies are coming anytime now." It is a smile from within. If cookies are coming, you aren't going to be grinning like a crazed maniac. You will have a relaxed, pleasantly happy face and await the arrival of the cookies.

If you lock eyes with anybody, nod. Nod, and in your head, telepathically say to them, "Cookies are coming."

This is what I did at that holiday party, and my girlfriend's peers came away with a great impression. She asked me, "What did you do that everyone liked you so much?"

I replied, "Cookies are coming."

This technique makes you look calm, confident, and approachable. So, when you do it, expect people to come up and start talking to you. Whenever I use this technique, people come over and talk. It's like magic. Use it and you are absolutely going to see results. Students of mine who have tried it absolutely love it.

I was at a concert by myself, and a group of three beautiful ladies came up and started talking to me. They sat with me through the show. I believe it was because of my Duke Cookie Face.

I was at a restaurant getting an order to go and, while I was waiting, Duke Cookie Face. Someone came up and started talking to me.

I met a lot of people. I made a lot of connections through this alone. This has served me so well, and it's minimum effort. If you go to a place and you're waiting, or if you are just out in the community and you do it, people will talk to you—you're open, you're giving an open vibe to communicate, you look friendly and approachable.

If you are at an event and you're sitting like that, you don't know who's looking at you. You never know who might be glancing over passing judgment on you, right? But this gives you a really good platform, so you might not even know someone's over there like, "Hey, so who's that person?" They look and they say, "Oh, they look confident, approachable, friendly, and..." They might not talk to you, but they will notice you and come away with a good impression. Assuming once again you weren't messing with your phone.

You were open, with open body language, waiting patiently

for your cookies to arrive, right? You have the glow. Cookies are imminent.

People feel that energy.

So, it's one of the best moves. Master this. Master it and use it. Look in the mirror. Find what your cookie face is. What do I look like if I think cookies are coming? Hey, cookies are coming. You know, kind of a casual like, "Ah, my best friend is going to be giving me some cookies and I'm looking forward to that." Body language is open when sitting down.

You can also do it standing, but it is considerably more difficult. If you are going to do a standing Duke Cookie Face, make sure you get a lot of practice in.

All right, go find yourself a mirror and get your cookie face on!

IF I COULD SEE MYSELF

A friend of mine said, "I wish I could see myself in a social situation to see how I appear, how I look, to see if I look approachable, to see if I look awkward." And so, how would you do that? I told him this—the Duke Cookie Face we talked about is your best asset, since you can't see yourself but you can feel it, you can feel yourself, so you'll know that you look approachable. You'll know to pay attention to your posture. Shoulders back. If you do the cape technique, you're walking like you have the cape. If you're paying attention to your posture and do your cookie face, you won't look awkward, weird, or like a killer. You'll look approachable, confident, and calm.

And so, even though you can't see yourself, if you use these techniques, you're going to appear OK. You're going to be good. And, to answer my friend's question, the next best thing to being able to see yourself is to use the Duke Cookie Face, sitting or standing. You've got the Cape Walk as well. That's an excellent start; now let's add to it.

THE SCAN AND YOUR HANDS

All right, so you showed up at the event. You're there, you're inside. What do you do?

You know how you're supposed to walk and how you're supposed to sit. There are events where you're primarily sitting, and there are events where you're primarily standing for a while before you sit. Either way, it starts off the same because you're standing when you walk in. So as soon as you walk in, you're going to try to locate the drinks or food. Usually there will be some type of drinks or snacks. It might just be coffee, water, or something like that. And then if there's food, they might have little finger sandwiches or hors d'oeuvres of some sort.

You want to head straight to the food or drink area, so when you walk in, you're scanning.

How is it set up? Where are people gathered? If people are sitting, what is the arrangement of the tables? Who's at the tables already? Who's not? Is there a reserved seating situation?

You're taking that all in while you are heading over to where the food and/or drinks are.

You can even say to the first person you see, "This is a great setup! Where are the snacks?"

While you're walking to the food and/or drinks, you're trying to also scan to see if any of your pre-known people are there.

Once you arrive at the food and drink area, you will get yourself a drink. You don't have to actually drink it, but you need something in your hand. If there are no drinks or food available, then usually there is some literature, or you can carry a notebook to have something in your hand. The other hand you can keep free so you can shake hands and gesture, or you can have a pen in that hand. I like to have a pen and sometimes a 3x5 notecard, because I like to write stuff down.

Another thing you can get yourself is a saucer or napkin and hit up those little sandwiches; put three of them on there. And now that you have three, you can eat one and keep two for display purposes and walk around with that. Or, you have the drink AND the sandwiches if you are ambitious and walk around with both hands full. But this way at least you won't have to worry about what to do with your hands.

Your first opportunity to socialize will most likely be at the food area. Usually there are going to be other people over by the food. So, when you get there, you can ask about the sandwiches. "Oh, have you tried those? Which sandwiches are the best?" "Cucumber sandwiches?" "Interesting. Hey, did you try one of those?" "You like this?" "Is this sour cream or is it butter?" "That's delicious. I think I might try to make these at home. What's your favorite?" All good conversation starters.

Or, if you're already there and someone else comes up, you can say, "Try these. Try these. These cucumber ones with the—I think that's sour cream." "Sour cream?" "Yeah. I think it's a strange combination but it's delicious." Or, you could say, "Hey, I just come for the sandwiches. They know I like sandwiches, so they keep inviting me. I come to so many of these events I'm starting to put on weight."

There are all kinds of conversations or observations you can make about the food.

More examples of things to say: "Last time, they had giant

pretzels. I guess that didn't work out too well because they're not offering them this time."

Or…"Oh, only punch? Ah, I was expecting there to be a keg here. We could have done some keg stands."

Whether you are the first one there and people come over, or people are there, and you come up, you can always think of something to say about the food to engage them. If there's no one there to talk to, simply get your food or drink and move on. I'll tell you what to look for next.

"Hey, Nick, what if there's no food or drinks there? What am I supposed to do then?"

Have a pen in your hand, or maybe some kind of notebook, something to take notes on for the event. And then the other hand is available to gesture or shake hands.

Don't put your hands in your pockets. A lot of people put their hands in their pockets—don't do that. Keep your hands out of your pockets. Hold on to something. So, hopefully you'll have food or a drink, but if not, then a notebook or a pen, and you'll be good to go.

VOCAL INFLECTION

Let's talk about vocal tonality and vocal inflection. This is important because it tells the people around you and the person you are communicating with about how you see yourself and how they should see you in the hidden human hierarchy structure and in position to them.

So usually it comes off as you are either seeking approval, talking down to them, or using a neutral tone as peers would with one another.

This is something you need to pay attention to and work on. For example, if you are usually soft spoken but you need to be in command of the room for a particular situation, your message may not go over with the same weight that it should.

I try to make a deliberate effort to have my tone reflect that we are peers, even if someone is a big-time VIP or celebrity. For the most part, they seem to respect it more than if I were kissing up to them. People are people. But yes, you will come across some people who, the moment they arrive, begin by talking down to you. Usually you can prevent this if you have been doing your Cape Walk and remember to keep your shoulders down and back and have a confident duke/duchess cookie face on. I understand that sometimes you weren't prepared and were caught off guard, and now you are in a position where you slipped and need to regain your footing.

Usually once that relationship is established, it is difficult to change your status, but of course, there are ways to do it.

In the Air Force, there was a young man named Francisco. One day during our duties I told him to go and complete a list of tasks. He was in the process of smoking a cigarette. He looked off into the distance, took a deep drag off the cigarette, turned and looked me straight in the face, calmly blew the smoke out to the side, and said, "Okay, I'm going to do that, but...next time, ask me, don't tell me." The vocal pitch he carried was as though we were peers (we weren't peers, I outranked him). I remember thinking for a second, *Who does this guy think he is?*

Now you have to keep in mind this was the military and I could have "flexed on him." However, I respected his request. I thought, *I like this kid.* I ended up mentoring him, and he was a great guy. He went on to do some outstanding things.

The point is, you want to be aware of your vocal tone when you speak to people, because you are subconsciously telling them how to treat you. You are trying to get as much advantage as you can, and your body language is going to say a LOT, but we've covered that. Your vocal tone is going to speak volumes (pun intended), so you need to be aware of that too.

This takes a lot of practice, so you can't expect to be good at it immediately. You have to pay attention, be in the moment, and make a conscious effort of it. Once you do it a few times, it feels really good and you'll start doing it more and more. But you always need to pay attention and practice when you can.

It makes a big difference when you are out and about in the workplace or doing business deals, or even dating. Shoot for that "we are peers" tone, and you'll notice the results. This is one of those exercises where the results and feedback are visible to you very quickly.

My mother got bullied by her cousins growing up. Now they are all old, "senior citizens," and still when they get together, my mother takes this really subservient tone with them. They still try to get at her while she seeks their approval.

Naturally, this bothers me. And I hope they read this book because I don't approve of them treating my mother this way. I don't speak to them to seek approval like my mother does. I speak to them as peers, and I believe I'm respected and recognized as such.

My recommendation to you is to speak to people as though you are peers regardless of the circumstance.

Do it with the service people, maids, handyman, pool boy, waiter, and do it with the VIP guests and celebrities as well. It's respectable and will make you respectable.

"But how do you do it, Nick? You say to do it, but you don't say how."

Here's how. Mindset changes tone. Posture changes tone. Mood changes tone. Thinking of these three things, I consider my circumstances, select the mood, or at least notice the mood, and select the proper posture. Then for the mindset part I either tell myself this is one of my peers disguised and acting as this other person so I can talk to them that way. Or I think, *who do I know that would be good at speaking in this situation?* And I invoke them. I talk like I imagine they would in this scenario. Give that a try.

HUNTING INTROVERTS

Next, you are going to be looking for introverts. You're hunting introverts. You're looking for people like you; you'll be able to spot them. There are always going to be introverts—you'll see them, usually around the fringes, because that's where you would normally be, right? You'd be around the edges. So, you're going to look for people who look like you feel. There is a high likelihood that they may be messing with their phone, acting like, "Oh, I'm a little busy here because this is very interesting on my phone," but you know that's a bunch of bull. They are just messing with their phone because they don't know what else to do.

Or they'll just be kind of sitting there with their food or

drink, just looking nervously around or down or at some literature, nibbling. And so, you'll spot them.

You know what it's like because you're one of them. I'm one of them, so I can spot these people. You're hunting introverts, so you're going to go over to them. Go get that introvert! You have "first mover" advantage, so you are coming in from a position of strength.

Even if you're a little nervous, you're the hunter. Let them be the nervous one because they don't know that you're coming. Walk up and engage, "Hey, how's it going? How are you this evening? Pretty good? Did you try the cucumber sandwiches?

Or..."Last time, they had cucumber sandwiches, but there's no food this time. I wonder what happened?"

And so, you "open" that introvert. You talk to them. They're going to be very happy that you're there. They're going to be very happy to see you, because they were just standing/sitting there waiting, waiting to be rescued. You're a hero! Act like it!

Now, with your new friend, you have the power of two.

Start talking and see if they seem interesting. They probably won't be. Either way, try to learn something.

You can learn something from everybody you meet. Don't ask them what they do. They'll tell you eventually. Introduce yourself and bring up some observations about the event, about the food, about the drinks, or about the venue. You will start with just observational conversation. "Did you notice this?" "What do you think about this?" "Are you from out of town?" "I noticed you have an accent. What accent is that?" Things like that. But remember, don't ask them what they do. The key here is, you are no longer alone. It's you and them, the power of two, and that's a good place to start.

MORE PEOPLE TO TALK TO AT EVENTS

I mentioned that you should hunt introverts and speak with them, but there are also some other people you should add to your list when you are deciding who to engage with at an event.

I don't always get the opportunity to do it, but I like to try to talk to who I think is the oldest person at the event, the youngest person, and the person I least want to talk to (at any event there is always someone you spot and you immediately judge them and think, *I absolutely don't want to talk to that person*, so I make sure to talk to that person). The reason is, they are there too, and once you start doing this, you usually find out that it is good that you ended up talking to that person. You judged them and deemed them unworthy of your conversation, but you could have been wrong. Oftentimes you will be wrong, and sometimes you will be right. You'll walk away and think, *I knew I shouldn't have talked to that guy.*

Then there is usually someone in the room who looks like a killer. It might be the same person that you didn't want to talk to. Talk to them. Then look for the person who looks like they don't fit in and talk to them too. So, for example, if it is a formal event and someone is underdressed, or they're wearing a suit that looks too big for them, or they have bad fashion sense, or they seem really out of place, talk to them. They are usually awesome. However, sometimes they suck. But at least you'll know.

Remember, you are there, and they are there. Step up and engage.

THE MAGIC OF THREE

When you walked in and went over to the food, if you recognized somebody there, you have more options. Instead of hunting for introverts right away, go to the person you are pre-known with and say, "Oh, hey..." If you only know them from online, introduce yourself.

"But Nick, what if they are already talking to someone?" Simple, you just stand there quietly next to them with your Duke Cookie Face, and then they will eventually notice you're standing there and they will engage. (Naturally use your judgment to see if it looks like it is a serious conversation or something light before you invade their space.) Introduce yourself, "Hey, I'm Nick from the online forum" (or wherever you know them from). But if you have met them or went out for beers with them the night before, then you're actively looking for them, and they'll probably be looking for you. You get your sandwich, then go directly over to them, or if you see them when you first walk in, do a quick intro and then say, "I'm going to grab a snack really quick. I'll be right back." Get your snack and return. Now you're two people standing there socializing.

I'd like to introduce you to what I call "The Magic of Three." Three is the perfect number. If you are in a group of two, you want to get a group of three. Four is too many because it allows you to default into nothingness.* In a group of four, there is always someone just sitting there quietly watching everyone else; it's too easy to blend in. In a group of four, there's going to be one person who shines, and the rest don't really get to know each other. So, you want a group of three.

*(If you are a couple and talking to another couple, then four is fine.)

So, if you find yourself in a two-person group, get your basic conversation started, but keep in mind, you're going to want to grab another one.

Pay attention to the person you are talking to but also keep a watchful eye. If you see someone walking by who looks like they might be interesting to talk to, you can pull them in like, "Hey, let's grab this guy." And you gesture toward them to join you and bring them in to whatever you're talking about. "Hey, we're just talking about the sandwiches." And now you have three.

Look for people who are strolling by but not walking with purpose. They are just sort of moseying along. They will be good choices as they secretly want to be rescued, so they will be happy to join your group.

Now, the cool thing about the group of three is that the conversation can be much smoother. Nobody has to champion the conversation. It is easy to throw in your input and share your views with one another. Usually one person in the group might not be interesting to you and the other person might. Now you have a choice on who you focus on. If your initial person is not interesting, you're still learning from them, but you might bring this other person in so you can both divert your attention and focus on them. Plus, when you are talking, if you start running out of stuff to say, this third person can, and most likely will, chime in.

The conversation goes a lot more smoothly if there are three. However, the biggest benefit is that you can always leave if you want to, and it will be smooth and easy to do so. If you want a break or to simply meet other people, it's easier to leave if there are three because then those two are still together talking. You're in the three and you can say, "Oh, excuse me," and leave them talking. They're still good. They're cool. If you're just with one person, you're like, "Well, I'm going to leave." It's much harder to just walk away and leave them standing there alone. If there are three of you, you can always leave to go hunt another introvert, grab another person, etc.

Let me add in here that if you came with someone, it's a little different scenario because then you only need to grab one person. You can go in, look around, and say, "Oh, there's one. We'll get this guy." If it's a pre-known person, that's cool, and if not, then grab a random introvert and you're set!

However, like I said earlier, if you are a couple, you can always match up with another couple and do the four-person grouping.

Also, a good thing if you arrived with a plus-one is to split off from whoever you came with after you have your third person and it gets flowing pretty well. You'll get back together once it's time to sit down, assuming there's a sit-down part.

But for the stand-up networking part, it's better. You can meet a lot more people if you split.

Just be sure to get that third person first then split off and leave your plus-one talking to them, and hopefully they'll grab another to make their new group of three. You break off. Go and make another group of three of your own over here. Then if you meet someone you think would be cool to introduce to your plus-one, you say, "Hey, you've got to meet so-and-so." Then you take them over there and vice versa.

They will do the same for you, so you can cover a lot more area and your chances of meeting that one person you're trying to meet and really connect with are multiplied.

If you showed up at the event alone, you could also look for people who showed up as a pair. There might be a husband and a wife, there might be two friends, or there are just people who know each other and they're already a pair. You can usually go up to the pair, especially if it's a husband and wife. I love those teams because they talk to each other all the time, so they are probably looking forward to talking to someone new. It's easy because they are a pair already and you're the third. You go up to them and say, "Hey, what's going on? How are you two?"

Or hit them with the observations, "Hey, this is what I noticed." "What do you think about those cucumber sandwiches?" "Is that cream cheese? Sour cream? Or is that butter?" "How high do they stack the cucumbers in there? Is it like a double layer or what?"

There's no shortage of things you can talk about. (I know you're thinking, *What's up with this guy and cucumber sandwiches?* Well if you must know, I noticed that they have cucumber sandwiches at way too many events, and I'm always confused by it, because I never remember anyone ever saying they liked them.)

You still have the option to leave the two people and create another group of three or join another pair and become a group of three. Always be on the lookout for the advantage.

The Magic of Three is really powerful. It's a really good thing. If there's already a group of three, don't try to jump in and be the fourth person. It's really good to either grab someone, make it two, and then grab someone else to make it a three-person group, or join their pair and become a group of three. Or if you arrive with somebody, grab one other person and make it three people. Three is your magic number. Work with that. Thank me later.

THE BACKUP PLAN

What if you show up to an event and you do not see the introvert around the edges? They're not there. You're looking, but you're not finding them. What if you don't see the pair, the husband and wife team? Or just the two friends who are sitting there who look welcoming, like they're waiting for you to join?

I bring this up because this actually happened. This happened to me! And I thought, *This is highly unusual. The situation that is always the case is now suddenly not the case. Uh oh!*

My mistake. I wasn't early. I showed up around half an hour after the start. There were a bunch of people there, and they were already in groups of four or more.

Everyone seemed to know each other, and there were no side stragglers. It was nothing like I had previously described. And so, what do you do if you show up and you're just like, *Well, I can't hunt introverts. I don't see any. I don't see the husband and wife team. I don't see any two people who seem like they're bored. And there's not one person looking at their phone that I can go up and talk to.* What do you do in that scenario?

First thought I had was, *Maybe I should just leave.*

But no, I couldn't do that. I had to stay and figure it out. For me and for YOU. I had to put myself to the test. I knew there had to be a way. And...I figured it out.

Here's what you do. You were invited by a host. The host is obligated to talk to you. So, in my case, I looked over. The host was over by the door. And as people were walking in, the host was greeting them and telling them the layout of the event.

I walked over to the host. His name was Patrick. So, I went over and said, "Hey, Patrick. How's the night treating you so far? Your event is kicking ass, man! Looks like you've got a good turnout." And I gestured to the crowd.

He proceeded to talk with me but was also welcoming people as they came in.

He was welcoming people as they entered, and I was standing next to him.

Pay attention to this part.

So, he welcomed them and shook their hands, then naturally they turned to me, because I was standing next to him, the host.

I welcomed them and shook their hands. "Hey, I'm Nick. Nice to meet you. Thanks for coming out."

So, what happened? People arriving were greeted by the host, they knew him, and they saw that I was standing next to him. They assigned in their minds some kind of event status to me because I was there with the host and I also greeted them as they arrived.

"Hey, nice to meet you. Enjoy."

In their minds, I was linked somehow to the host or the event.

I stood there with Patrick and welcomed about ten people. Some were in groups, and some were in couples. I don't think anyone came by themselves.

I figured ten people was a good start, so I turned to the host, thanked him for the invite, and told him I'd catch up with him later.

Now, since I had just met ten new people, and they were just getting settled in at their tables with their drinks and stuff, I was able to just go over, sit down, and start opening conversations with them. Since they had just met me with the host, they were like, "Oh, this is Nick. We just met him." And so, the work was done, and it was a lot easier to go and socialize now that I was "known."

So, if you should find yourself in this scenario, hang out by the host, with the host. As people are coming in, introduce yourself. All those people you are meeting are eligible to go follow up with; just don't wait too long. Stay fresh in their memory as they're getting settled in. Go over there and open a conversation with them. And that's how it's done.

BODY LANGUAGE CHECK

Sure, there's a lot of stuff happening around you, but whenever you can, remember your body language. Remember you're walking like you have a cape. Remember to check your shoulders; they should be down and back. Remember to try to keep the cookie face going. Remember your posture; it's OK to slip, but when you remember, correct it.

You want to be standing or sitting straight but relaxed, open body language, not messing with the phone. Maybe hold your drink, napkin, or saucer with food, and add the cookie face representing the duke or duchess within you. Cool? Cool.

The more you practice, the more it will become a natural part of you when you are in these situations.

SUMMARY

Let's review. Your expectations are to make one meaningful, good connection. One. You're trying to get one. If you can do that, success. If you can't do that, it's still a success because you will have learned something.

You're trying to find someone you genuinely like, would like to have as a friend, and really feel a connection with. You'd like to learn and know more about them. And they most likely feel the same about you. That's what you're ultimately looking for. You're not trying to sell anybody anything. You're just trying to make a true, real connection with somebody.

How to dress: remember, you don't have to get super fancy, but you want to at least hit the standard and then have maybe an accessory that is unique and stands out a little bit, or just dress up a level higher than everyone else.

Be early. Make sure you're early so then you get the lay of the land and you can really choose how you're going to take care of things, how you're going to set up and watch people come in. It's easier for you to go and approach people as they're coming in because they're not settled in yet. They're just coming in. You're settled and you can observe and be observed much more easily. If it's primarily a sitting event where you sit at tables and you're one of the first at the tables, you can sit there with your Duke Cookie Face and gesture to people to come join you. You're the king or queen—oh, sorry, "duke or duchess"—of the table already. You're situated much better than walking in late, looking for an open spot, and just settling to sit wherever. You get more choices if you're early.

No phone play. Put that phone away. Put it on silent or leave it in the car. Do not pull out that phone. Don't do it. Don't do it—it will really handicap your ability to network.

Duke Cookie Face—we talked about that. You're going to sit like a duke or duchess, and your face is going to be like "cookies are imminent, cookies are coming." You're excited about it, you're happy about it, but not like a crazy person—more like a quiet satisfaction on your face. It makes you very open and approachable, you look confident, and you look like you know what you're doing.

The Cape Walk—remember when you're walking, it's like you have a cape and you want it to flow in your wake. That will ensure you have a good walk because you want your imaginary cape to have a proper drape to it when you move. You don't want it like a flag flapping in the wind. You want the cape to flow.

The Magic of Three—three is the perfect number that you want to have when you're networking and socializing, because it is way easier to actually be noticed, be in the conversation, and keep it flowing if there are three. It's much better than two. And if somebody's a little boring, still try to learn from them. However, it's better if there's another person because then they can take a little bit of the tension off and it keeps the conversation going. Maybe this person has something to say. Maybe you can angle to them. Plus, you can leave more easily and start another group of three. Three is perfect. Four is a little too much. If you show up with one person, if you have a plus-one, then you're going to look for one to get your group of three. If you show up by yourself, you can look for a couple, or you can get one person and then snag another one, hunting the introverts.

Hunting introverts: when you go in, you're looking for people like you. You're looking for introverts. You can usually spot them, especially if you're early, as there will be some there early and they'll be lingering around the sides, usually on their phone. It is your duty to go in there. Get them. Rescue them, then get situated with your drink so you have something to do with your hands. Get settled in with your food, your drink, your pen in your hand, or whatever. Don't put your hands in your pockets. Engage the introverts. You are the hunter. You get to control how this goes. It's better than someone coming and grabbing you. You go get them.

If all else fails, if the host invited you, they're obligated to talk to you. You can approach them if nothing else has worked out. You can always go over there and hang out with the host for a little bit. Naturally don't bug them too much because they are busy hosting, but you can be over by them and talk to them now and then. And as people are coming in and talking to the host, usually somebody will come in who'll say something interesting or trigger something in you. You might think, *Oh, this seems like an interesting person. I think I'd like to talk to them more.* Then you part from the host and go engage that person. So, if all else fails, do the host method. It's good to have options, right?

Chapter Four

NETWORKING

Networking, socializing, connecting—that's where we're at now. This is where the rubber meets the road. This is when you're trying to connect, and so I'm going to show you some steps, what to do, what to say, how to navigate around the actual networking. We got you all the way up to this point to prepare you for this moment, and now let's get to it. Let's network!

WHAT NOT TO SAY

Normally, when people network, they do so on autopilot and have automatic programmed things they do. Almost everyone does it. They introduce themselves and then say, "What do you do?"

"Hey, Nick! I'm Mike. I'm an oral surgeon in Atlanta. What do you do?"

This sucks. I always say don't do it. The reason I say don't do it is because everyone does it. If you do it, you are almost surely going to have an unremarkable, forgettable interaction with this other person. Your goal is to set yourself apart. You're trying to stand out and be remembered. And if you do what everyone else is doing, then you're going to get the same results everyone else is getting.

People aren't going to remember you like I remember the Hawaiian shirt guy. They will just respond with their automatic responses. Everyone has automatic responses when people ask them the same questions. Think about when people ask you these questions—you most likely just throw out some preprogrammed thing and just go through the motions. I have been noticing that when I take an Uber ride, the drivers almost always default to a conversation about the weather. Well, OK...you're not going to learn anything interesting that way. If you are doing the same programmed conversation that everyone else is doing, you become invisible. You want to be *visible*. You want to be seen!

So, we're going to get into different things you can say in a moment. But what do you do if somebody asks you what you do? And believe me, they will.

Here are some options for you.

If you really enjoy what you do—for example, you are a

rocket scientist and you really enjoy being a rocket scientist PLUS you want to talk about being a rocket scientist—then say, "Hey, I'm a rocket scientist."

Wow, Nick! You're a genius! Share more of your wisdom with us!

Research suggests that many people aren't really super into their jobs. They have their titles—I'm a this, I'm a that. But if you want to be *real*, you're going to want to change it up a bit. For me, that would mean not just saying, "I'm a petroleum chemist."

Someone might say, "Great!" But then they want to talk about petroleum chemistry with me...I don't want to talk about petroleum chemistry. I have absolutely no desire to talk about that, so if they start talking about that, I'm going to excuse myself and avoid them for the rest of the event.

I would like to talk about something else. So, if I say that's what I do, I could very well end up in a conversation where I'm talking about something I don't want to be talking about. And that's going to suck for them and for me.

So, here's what I do when they come up and ask, "Hey, what do you do?"

I would say, "Petroleum chemist, but my main passion project right now that I'm working on is making a documentary about trying to reverse-engineer becoming a local celebrity in Brazil."

And so, in that way, I'm shifting it. I throw it down. I state—this is what I do, but then, this is what I'm passionate about. This is what I'm working on...because I want to shift to talk about that thing. And so, one of the things you might say to somebody is, "What interesting projects are you working on?" "What cool project do you have?" "What's the latest and greatest with you?" "What is the best vacation or the coolest recent vacation you took? Do you have any suggestions?" "What's a cool restaurant? Or, what's a great meal that you've had recently?" "Did you have any terrible meals this week? Tell me about *that.*"

And then once you get somebody rolling, if you're listening, you can pick something out for follow-up questions and you can learn something. We're going to get more into that in a bit. But the main point is not to ask people what they do. You're going to learn what they do. You'll find out what they do over time.

They're going to tell you (usually). It's most likely going to come out in conversation. But more importantly, you're going to hear what they are interested in, what they're passionate about, what projects they're working on. That's what they want to talk about. That's what you really want to learn about them, because if they're a dentist or something and they don't like talking about dentistry, but you're asking them questions about dentistry, then it's a no-win for everybody.

A LITTLE BIT MORE

If you don't have a fancy title and you're just a regular dude (like me), don't act like you're more important, richer, or know something more than you know. Don't try to elevate yourself and fake it, because people are going to see through that right away. This happens all the time. If you want to make sure that you are not going to be making any good connections, then go ahead and do that. Just remember, you are here to make good connections and to network and establish some real friendships and connections with people, so you're going to want to be authentic.

So, for example, I go to my fair share of polo events. I don't really know anything about polo, so I'm not going to engage in polo conversation like I know what's going on. But I can ask questions. It's great! People like to teach you about stuff, so if you say, "I come to these, but I don't know anything about this. Do you know something about this? What exactly is happening here?" When you ask questions, somebody will be happy to educate you and share their knowledge. They're not going to be like, "Oh, you don't know? Why are you here? Get out!"

No. They will be happy to be the teacher and inform you about it because it's also an ego thing. People like feeling needed. And honestly, you need their knowledge.

Plus, the ambiance is really cool, and there's always good cocktails and cool people around.

A similar situation is when I go to a baseball game. I don't watch the game. I'm there to socialize, see the people, and just take in the atmosphere.

On occasion, I'll watch some of the game. But that's not what I'm there for. The point is: don't act like you are something you're not.

I don't act like I'm super wealthy, and I don't act like I have knowledge that I don't have and/or that I'm super important. Try to keep it understated—you're trying to be remembered and stand out, but you're not trying to be remembered as a douche bag.

When people ask you about yourself, most people are like, "I am the director of..." "I'm the CEO of..." People want to flex their titles so they can show how important they are so that maybe you'll respect them, but usually it ends up making them look like a douche bag. Some of the people you meet at these places are actual big shots for real, so don't get into a pissing match about your title.

I recommend doing the opposite. It's worked amazingly well for me.

You can just say something like, "I'm Nick Shelton. I'm just a regular dude, just some guy who likes sandwiches."

It catches people off guard, so they instantly become more curious. They're like, "Regular guy? So, Nick, what is it that you do?"

"I'm just some random dude, doing random dude stuff, nothing noteworthy or worth mentioning."

And then they're like, "Huh?" Because they're so used to people trying to throw out fancy titles, when you just say, "I'm a regular guy," they really get curious. They think, *What does he do? He must be kind of important because he is trying to understate what he does.*

There is power in not trying to flex a title and not trying to be important. I always understate what I do because it is more fascinating and memorable that way.

So, you could say that you're "just a regular guy" or "I'm just some lowly nobody in the oil and gas industry, hardly worth mentioning. A dog with a note tied to it could do my job." And then they're like, "Huh? Well, that's probably not true."

All they know is that you're at the same high-level event with them, so they will really step up the questions to try to figure you out, and that is when you can talk about your project or whatever you actually want to talk about. "Enough oil and gas talk. Here's what I'm working on. This is what's interesting to me." And you're going to want to put your interest out there. We're going to talk about that next.

YOUR INTERESTS

Putting your interests out there. Why is that important? It's important to let people know what you're interested in and what you like because it opens up a lot of different possibilities.

It opens up invitations to do a lot of cool stuff, because as you are meeting people, you don't know who these people may know, and you don't know what they have access to. And, if you become friends and you're their friend and they're your friend, you will remember if they have an interest. Maybe they once said, "I've always been fascinated about beekeeping."

And maybe your cousin has this huge farm of bees and invites you to go harvest honey one day or something. Then you'd think, *Oh, I'll call up Clyde because I remember he said he was fascinated about stuff like that. Maybe he'd like to come*

along and check out this honey harvest. I think he'd get a kick
out of it.

And the same goes the other way. For example, I love sail-boats. So, in my conversations with someone new, I will almost always bring up the fact that I love sailboats. "Hey, I love sailboats, yachts, and ocean kayaking."

I don't really know a whole lot about how to sail, but I love being on a sailboat any chance I get. And so, by putting that "out there," people know, "Oh, it's Nick. He loves sailboats."

My buddy Jerry's father just so happens to have a sailboat, and he does sailboat racing in the Gulf of Mexico. One day, one of his crew did not show up because they were sick and couldn't make it for this particular race.

His dad was looking for a replacement, and Jerry said, "Nick likes sailboats. He would probably like this." They called me up and asked, "Hey, you want to crew in a sailboat race?" I said, "Yes, absolutely!"

"The only problem is, I don't know how to do that actually. I have never crewed a racing yacht before."

He said, "Can you do what I tell you to do?"

"Yes."

"Okay. Come on. Let's go!"

And I got to have that experience, one of the best memories of my life! But that's only because I put my interest out there, they knew what I was interested in. So when an opportunity came up, they said, "Oh, Nick would probably be interested in this." "Hey, do you want to come out?" "Yes, I do."

And the same with you—you want to put your interests out there. When people put their interests out to you, you can do the same to them. Because it might be really easy for you to have access to something that is difficult for someone else to have access to. You might be able to be that connection, that line for them to have an experience they will remember forever.

So, remember when you're having conversations with someone new, put your interest out there and let people know what you're into. People bond over similar interests, so don't keep that to yourself. Share it. They might share the same interest or know someone else who does.

ACTIVE LISTENING

Be an active listener. This is something that we, introverts, usually excel at.

How do you actively listen? Simple, you listen fully—not

the type of listening where you are waiting for them to stop talking so you can say your part. Actually sit/stand there and listen.

People will notice and pick up the fact that you are actually listening.

Think about it. There are times when you are talking, and you know people hear you but probably aren't listening, and then there are other times when you are positive they *are* listening. You want them to feel that way when they are talking to you.

But what if they are boring? Listen to them, too, until you can eventually make your escape. Until then, you're going to be the person who's actually going to listen. Listen like what they are saying is important, and you're going to learn something actually useful. By listening fully and actively, you're going to hear some stuff that you will have follow-up questions about.

However, when they stop talking, you will first want to repeat a summary of what they said back to them to be sure you understood, and it also shows you were listening, and then follow up with any questions.

What are the right questions? Well, most likely it will be something along the lines of, "I wonder about this." "What happens if this?" Or, "When you do that, what about this?" "Did you ever think about this?" "How does it feel when you do that?" "And did this ever happen?"

And so, there are all kinds of things and, once again, when people are talking, they love it when people are actually listening and paying attention to them.

Even if it's boring or a subject you don't care about, you should still try to learn at least one new useful thing.

And so, be an active listener and you will get your turn to talk as well, or maybe not; maybe you'll just listen. But they'll remember you because you'll be the person who listens and asks questions. So, after your first intro and you're in your group of three, to whoever is talking, listen and listen more. Be an active listener. Less talking, more listening, and then when there is a space for a follow-up question, ask your follow-up questions.

EASY CONVERSATION HACKS

"Nick, when I'm talking with people, what am I supposed to talk about?"

Everyone wants to know about conversation starters and all the hacks and tricks of actually talking to people.

Well, there are a lot of books about how to do that. There are a lot of techniques. There's even a deck of cards you can buy that have conversation starters on them.

But when I was building my network, I didn't have any of those tools. I didn't have the books and the decks of cards that say, "Hey, ask this, ask this."

So, if you want, you can get yourself a book on conversation starters or a card deck that has icebreakers on it. And that's fine.

I prefer a different way. I don't want to have to memorize anything. I need to be able to operate on the fly under all conditions.

What do I use to start my conversations? Usually I stick with observations.

You are observing things about the venue, about the event, and about the people you are talking to. So, it's really easy to pick out something. "I thought they were going to have sandwiches, but they don't have the sandwiches," or, "Hey, they have the sandwiches. Is that cream cheese or is that butter? Are you lactose intolerant? I don't understand lactose intolerance. I tolerate lactose just fine."

There is really no limit to the things you can say.

Or, you know somebody might have that belt or some accessory. "I like that belt. What's going on with the belt? I know there's a story with that belt, Todd." And you know this could be something about what they're wearing or something about pretty much anything—it's just observations.

You're looking around and your mind is going to notice stuff—you just have to remember what you noticed and then bring it up in conversation. "Hey, look, what do you think is going on over there with that?" "Hey, did you check out the men's room? There's actual art in there! This place is classy!" There's always something that you can bring up like, "Oh, I didn't know we were supposed to wear hats. Everyone has hats on. This is a hat thing, apparently. I didn't get the email. Someone should have told me about the hats."

There are all kinds of different things you can observe about the person. "Cool eyeglass frames, man. I like those. You're like a GQ model or something." There are all kinds of things you can say about what you're observing. And so, you have an unlimited source.

Just look around and then make a comment about something you see or notice.

Then there are the short stories. If it is relevant, if you have a short story about something you experienced or that fits with the theme of whatever somebody is talking about or what they observed, feel free to share that short story.

Keep it short and hit the highlights. Cut all the fat off because you don't need to drone on and on with long stories with people who just met you. But if it's interesting, or if it is some story you've told before and people have laughed and enjoyed it, and you see how it could fit and be relevant in this situation, tell the story.

Now for those who have spent time around me, you might say, "But you don't keep your stories short—you drag on and on." Yes, this is true, but my stories are awesome!

Questions. You might have some questions in your mind and say, "I don't know if I should ask this." Ask it. Ask the question!

It's kind of like the observations thing, but you can just ask questions about something you observed, or you can ask about whatever they said.

I talked about this earlier: whatever they've said, pick something out of that and ask a question about it. So, these are all things you can say that you don't have to memorize. You just observe and ask a question. State something about an observation. "It's like eighty-five degrees in here. Hmm. I wonder if that's some kind of technique to get us sweating, you know?"

And I think from that, I would follow up with something like, "In the movies in the '80s, the guys used to turn the thermostats up when they had girls over, and the girls would say, 'Oh, it's so hot in here,' and start taking their clothes off. But in real life, that doesn't work because I tried, and the girls just leave when you do that."

See, short little story. Bam! And then people are like, "Huh! Interesting." So, there's always some kind of way to slide a story in.

Now, I like to also throw in an embarrassing story and be vulnerable.

Telling an embarrassing story will always give you something to talk about. You tell the story and then there will usually be questions, and you can always reference back to the story later on as well. So, if I can, if there's something relevant and embarrassing that happened to me, I'll tell it. It's great to show a little vulnerability. If you are vulnerable first, people usually open up to you. You have to share something. You can't just be like, "Nope, everything is fine, smooth, and trouble free with me all the time. I'm a man (or woman) of steel. I'm just super strong. Nothing fazes me!"

People will pick up on that vibe. They'll feel you've got your guard up, and so in turn, they'll keep their guard up.

But if I say, "Hey man, I was over there by the sandwiches and I was thinking, 'Don't choke. Don't choke while you're eating this sandwich,' and I started choking. And it was kind of embarrassing because I'm like, 'Am I going to choke over here at this food table on this cucumber sandwich? I don't want to give the international sign or whatever for choking and have someone gave me the Heimlich maneuver and make them a hero because then I'm going to have to leave.' So, it's either, 'Am I going to be embarrassed?' or 'Am I going to die right here on the floor in front of these beautiful women, choking on a cucumber sandwich?'"

And when I was telling this story, people are like, "What did you do?"

"I gave myself the self-Heimlich over the back of the chair, and so I suppose, I'm the hero. I'm here, I'm alive, we can now enjoy this event! Glad I didn't have to put you through that scene of me choking over there and ruin the party for everyone."

That's a true story by the way. So, there are little stories you can share with people like that about something embarrassing that either happened to you at the event, before the event, or years ago that you can tie into what's going on now.

If you can be vulnerable and share something embarrassing, it really opens people up and they are more open to share things with you, talk to you, and let their guards down because they see you. They see you as a human being. You're not taking yourself too seriously. You're just a real person communicating and connecting with them, and it's all good.

USING NAMES IN CONVERSATIONS

I believe we have all heard this advice. We've been told that people love the sound of their own name so use it often in conversation. It makes sense, but I disagree, to a point.

Here is my opinion on the matter.

I agree that it is good to use a person's name in conversation but very lightly. When people use it a lot, it makes me instantly put my guard up because it sounds artificial, like they are trying to angle in on me or take advantage of me in some way.

If someone says, "Hey, Nick, it's a pleasure to meet you! So, Nick, how did that documentary you were shooting in Brazil turn out? That's so interesting. What would you say was the most rewarding thing about the experience, Nick? Really? That's so cool, that's really awesome, Nick! Listen, Nick, I'd like to speak with you more about this at the break if you have time, Nick, if that's cool? All right, Nick, I'll see you later!"

When people do that to me, I immediately feel like I need to get away from them. It is a red flag for me.

I would suggest perhaps using their name at the very beginning and then again at the end and that's it. So, "Nice to meet you, Nick," and "All right, Nick, it's been a pleasure. See you later."

To me, that is the perfect amount. Anything more seems strained and artificial.

DON'T SHALLOW NETWORK

Here's a very important and quick what-not-to-do when you're networking. I see it all the time and it pisses me off. I'm sure it pisses off a lot of other people too. Don't be one of these people.

So, there was a woman, a very beautiful woman who was at an event I attended. I met her. She came up and said, "Hi, I'm so-and-so, and you are?" I introduced myself and she said, "What is it that you do, Nick?" And I said what I did. And she said, "Oh, OK, nice to meet you. I'm going to meet some other people." Then she went through the room and systematically met everyone that way.

After meeting everyone, she tried to talk to only the people she felt could directly elevate and impact her business. If she didn't think you were in that category, she would ignore you.

It was really obvious to everyone what this woman was trying to do—she was there to just pick out "who's valuable to me" in this event to meet them and try to use them to further her business.

I will completely block you out if I find out you're that type of person. And there are a lot of other people who will do the same because no one wants to be around a person like that.

However, a LOT of people network that way. Don't do it!

You might wonder why you shouldn't network like that, because it seems to make sense to do it that way, right? You are trying to make connections that can improve your life and business, so why not streamline it and concentrate on talking to the specific people who can make that happen?

Here is the flaw.

When you are meeting people this way, you are only getting surface information. You don't know who that person knows just from the introduction.

You don't know what resources I have and who I know. For example, I have a really broad, international network of people who do a lot of things. I'm very well connected. So, you might come up and have a really quick introduction with me and say, "Well, this guy can't possibly help me. I need someone else," and then go meet someone else. They, on the surface, might seem like a good fit, but I might have more connections in whatever you're looking for than that person. You didn't know that, and now you have slighted me.

And so, that woman was showing up just to try to leverage people and use them to further her pursuits. She wasn't there to really connect. And the people she thought she connected with didn't really connect all that well either. I know that because I was with those same people again at a different event later in the week, and we talked about her and how crappy and superficial she was. So, she was shut out. She didn't even get the help from the people she had selected because they recognized what she was doing, and she was not held in high regard.

You want to meet people and get to know them, connect with them as they are, as a person, not as an industry or something. You're not there to use people—you're there to really connect and get to know people. And if they are your friend down the road, they're going to know what you do and connect you to their network. For example, if you are talking to your friend and saying, "I'm working on this project, and I'm trying to find a good computer programmer. The program I'm trying to write is this and will do that. This is my vision." They might say, "Oh, I know a really good programmer. We had problems finding a programmer we could trust, and we found someone. We use this guy. I highly recommend him." And then you'll get the hookup.

I help people all the time, and people help me, but I don't meet them and try to use them for something. I meet them to connect. If I like them and they like me, we become friends, and friends help friends. If you see a way you can help your friend, you help them out, right?

And so, don't "shallow network," because you're going to piss off a lot of people, and you're not going to get very far with the people you do meet. They're going to say, "It's obvious this person just came up to me because they're trying to use me to get this particular resource for their business instead of trying to make a genuine connection."

So, absolutely do not meet people that way. Don't just meet and dismiss, meet and dismiss. Actually try to get to know people.

You can walk up and add value, but don't walk up and try to take value.

If you're getting to know someone and you realize, *This doesn't seem like someone I want to have as a friend*, but they have good business connections who can really help you, perhaps you can be acquaintances and still do business, or maybe you just need to move on.

I have people in my network that I don't hang out with, but I respect them and what they do, and I touch base with them from time to time.

Treat your network with care like it's an extension of your family. Sure, there will be different levels of relationship but, when you start out, be genuine and let it evolve into whatever it's going to be. You may not end up being friends, but at least you established the relationship correctly at the beginning.

Remember, especially if you are building a large network, you don't know who people know and who they're connecting with. So, don't go in with shallow pursuits. You're going to make real connections, and that's what you're here for... real connections. That makes all the difference.

MAKING THE MOST OF UNCOMFORTABLE SITUATIONS

People in uncomfortable situations are your friend. I know that sounds strange but check this out. This is a really good habit to put into practice.

I was at a wine event in Argentina, and I noticed there was one couple who brought their baby. The baby was a newborn or just a few months old, and that baby was screaming at the top of his lungs. They were the only ones who brought a baby. No one else brought a baby to this thing. I don't know what their circumstances were, but they were determined to not let having a baby stop them from enjoying a good wine festival. They brought him, and one thing was very clear: that baby was not happy. He was screaming his frustrations. I looked around, and everyone seemed a bit disturbed by it...and for a moment I thought out loud, "Who would bring a baby to this?"

But then, I thought, *I know they didn't plan this out*. In their minds, this was supposed to go smoothly. Needless to say, they weren't making a lot of friends.

I figured I'd embrace the awkward and go talk to them. So, I went up to their table, and the first thing they did was apologize for the baby. "I'm so sorry." And I was like, "Oh no. I don't care. Babies cry, that's sort of what they do. I'm not mad at you guys. I know you wanted to come and enjoy this. I'm Nick. Nice to meet you."

I became really good friends with that couple. We are still very good friends to this day, and it has been a number of years now. It all started from me noticing that they came to this thing and found themselves in an uncomfortable situation. In that moment, they needed a friend.

I knew they wanted to enjoy the event like everyone else, but they had hit a little rough patch.

When you see someone having a bit of a moment, it's really easy to go and network with them and bond over the situation. There was no guarantee that they were going to be cool, but it turned out they were. It was also really easy to talk to them because nobody else was coming anywhere close to them thanks to their demonic child.

They wanted to meet people, but it's a bit difficult when you have a wild banshee with you. The baby did calm down a little later, and then everything was good. And yeah, they were able to enjoy the event and get some socializing in as well. As I mentioned before, I still know that couple and see them from time to time. Great people.

You never know what might come out of these things. So always be on the lookout for somebody who might have gotten themselves into an uncomfortable situation in a social setting, where you can step in and stand out from the rest to be remembered because you were there to help out. Never hesitate to step in and be there for somebody who might need you. You never know when you may be on the other side of that gesture as well, so build up some good karma while you can.

NETWORKING WITH STUDENTS

This is really good if you can do it because some students grow up to become successful people later on. You're playing the long game. If you can make friends with students, maybe down the road they will grow up to become something. Now you know people in all these industries that you've built friendships and relationships with. It's a beautiful thing.

So, for example, I was in Nicaragua attending Spanish classes. There was a teacher at this school who was teaching English to a bunch of law school students.

He asked me, "Would you mind coming to the class to help some of my students practice their English conversations?"

I said, "Sure." So, I went, helped out, and made friends with those law school students while helping them with their English.

These friendships flourished as the years passed, and some became very successful lawyers, some became university professors, while the rest went into other professions and occupations. We're still friends and have been for a long time, so that really helps my network in that country. I put the time in, and it has paid off BIG TIME.

I got to know them as they sprouted out into the world. I was a resource for them because I was older and farther along in my life journey and had experience. I had the opportunity to be a bit of a mentor to some of them.

I would say, "Feel free to reach out and use me as a resource. Maybe I can help you out in some way. Let me know."

And so, as these people advanced through the ranks in their own lives, they'd say, "You know, I know this one guy. I know Nick." And they know I travel a lot, and they might be going somewhere. "I'm trying to do this; who do you know? Can you help me out here?"

And I'd say, "Yeah, yeah, yeah. What can I do? Where are you trying to go? Who are you trying to meet?"

If you just so happen to currently be a student, it's definitely easy to network with other students. If you are not a student, it's good to network with some as long as it's in a professional way.

You don't want it to be creepy or weird. But if it's something like this where you're volunteering, helping people with their language, or are a judge at their university competition, try to meet as many students as you can and help them out whenever you can because you never know. And if you can help them, you're helping a friend, a friend now and a friend in the future. People remember stuff like that. It's really good to have connections like that. So, if you have the opportunity, do it.

STUDENT NETWORKING EXAMPLE

I was on an airplane flight to New York. I was in first class, and sitting next to me was a student who was a junior at one of the local universities. He was going home for the summer. He asked me a bunch of questions about how I do what I do because he was running a business of his own and thought I might be able to help or answer his questions about certain topics, which I was able to do. We had a really good conversation.

Later, as we landed, I found out his family owned a chain of venues that were doing some really exclusive stuff with musicians playing shows that were really hard to get tickets to.

He said, "My family owns this, and since you're visiting friends in New York, I'd like to give you VIP tickets if you would like to come to a show tomorrow. How many people would you say are in your group? Maybe like six or something?"

I said, "Yeah, sure."

"Okay, you'll be my guest. You can come check out a show, and I want you to know I appreciate your help and meeting you. Whether you come to the show or not, let's keep in touch."

Amazing! You never know when you add value, when you meet people and help them out, what might happen. I still have this gentleman's number in my phone, and we bounce some questions back and forth from time to time or just say hi every now and then to catch up.

You never know who you might meet. This guy was a student. I was able to help him out. He was cool. You never know, but the point is, if there is somebody that you can help, if they ask you questions or you find yourself in a position where you might be able to add some value to them, do it. You never know where it might lead.

CONVERSATION NO-NO'S

Don't kiss anyone's ass.

If you are in these high-end networking events where there are a bunch of who's who, captains of industry, and people who have had a lot of success, don't go in there kissing people's asses.

If you meet some celebrities, don't kiss ass. You can be friendly, but you're all there. You're on the list. They're on the list. If I get an invite, I'm there, you're there. So, you don't have to be kissing anyone's ass. We're all there, we're all people. You don't get yourself a good level of respect if you go in kissing ass. And it just looks bad—it's not good for anybody.

So, what do you do? Just be a peer. These are your peers. When you show up at the luxury automobile dealership, when you show up at the art gallery, or the private museum showing, when you show up at the wine festival, or the fleet of private jets, or the yachting event, don't kiss ass. Just be there and be genuine—be yourself. Don't try to elevate yourself and try to be something you're not. You're on the list, too. You're there. You are peers. Treat these people like you treat everyone else, respectfully.

Everyone brings something to the table. It's different degrees. Somebody might be worth a lot of money, but you're bringing your own expertise of what you know and what you do. You all have something to offer, so these are your peers.

Another thing is, don't apologize. This is a big thing that I personally do too much, and I have to stop. Because after a good conversation with somebody, I tend to say something like, "I apologize for taking so much of your time."

Don't do that.

Don't apologize for talking with people—if they didn't want to talk to you, they would have cut the conversation short and found someplace to be other than talking with you. If they're talking to you for a long time, it's because they were interested in talking to you, listening to you, and interacting with you. So, don't apologize after your conversation.

Just have your conversation and say, "Thanks. Catch up with you soon," or something like that.

But don't apologize.

ENHANCED DATING OPPORTUNITIES

Enhanced dating? Well, if you're single, networking can help you meet people to date because you're out at these events. I think it's much better than online dating because with that you meet someone and it's like a job interview. You are trying to force the situation. Nobody can behave naturally and be themselves.

But, networking, if you're just out at an event, you're being yourself. You're meeting people in their natural habitat. You're simply enjoying the show or wherever you're at, and you're socializing, talking to people. You're not there to "be with" any specific person. You're just there engaging with a lot of people. They're watching you and seeing how you are in that environment, and you see how they are in this open environment. But there's no pressure because you're not together. You're just there.

And so, for example, if you are at the symphony and you meet someone, there's no pressure for you. You're not together. But then maybe after a few of these times, you say, "Hey, I have an extra ticket to this. Would you like to go with me?" And now, you're out. You're out, maybe on a date. You've seen them several times before this in a natural and neutral environment and shared social event experiences.

You're much more relaxed because you've been around this person. You kind of know them, you kind of felt them out, they kind of see how you are, and they know what your interests are, because they've been around you in a no-pressure environment.

Now, you can go out, just the two of you, to some other things. It's like you've already known each other because you have built a light relationship in a much more comfortable way than if you just showed up as strangers and tried to force a date.

So just something to think about, and this works for men and women—just showing up, being around, and meeting people. Whatever you're into, you're meeting people you might be interested in and they might be interested in you. There's no obligation, and you don't have to act a certain way or try to peacock or be funny or anything like that. You're just there enjoying yourself, and they're there. You can meet a lot of people this way.

Also, through introductions, you might meet someone who could be a good match for you, too.

If that's what you're looking for, this is a good way to do it without having to really put in any extra effort. You are meeting people anyway, and from the people you meet, you just might happen to meet someone who is a good match romantically for you.

Here is another example of how your network can enhance your dating opportunities.

I wanted to attend a corporate holiday party, and this particular year, the one I normally attend was canceled. I, however, was still determined to go to one. I put the word out to my local network. "If you know anyone who needs a date to their corporate holiday party, I will gladly volunteer myself to accompany them."

Before the sun went down that day, I had a confirmed date to a corporate holiday party.

HOW TO LEAVE

How do you leave an event properly? Because you're in there, you're socializing, hanging out, and talking to people. For me, it's always so difficult to leave because I know it's going to take half an hour to shake everyone's hands and say, "Oh, it's been great!"

Then I just get roped back in.

So, what I like to do if it's warm weather, I'll just go to the bathroom. Yes, I actually go to the bathroom—I excuse myself, go to the bathroom, use the bathroom, and then when I come out of the bathroom, I just leave. I just walk out. Just walk out to the car and leave.

I might tell the host I'm leaving. It just depends on how big the function is. If it's a pretty big function, I won't usually tell the host unless they're really convenient and close by. But if they're busy or something like that, I'll just leave and then text the host to say, "I had a good time."

If it's wintertime, you have your coat and a bunch of winter gear, so for you to leave, you have to put it on while everyone is watching you put on all your stuff. If you smoke cigarettes or something, you would get a pass; nobody would even suspect. You'd simply go to smoke and then leave. But if you're not a smoker, then you actually have to tell the people in the area who are watching you put your coat on that you're leaving.

So, in warm weather—I'll just go to the bathroom and leave. And that's it. People will say, "I guess he left." And if it's cold weather, I will tell the people, "I'm taking off. It's been a pleasure meeting you. I'll be in touch." I talk to whoever is in the immediate area and then go. If I see the host or somebody on the way out, or somebody contacts me while I'm on the way out, I will say bye to them as well, but if not, I just slither on out of there and then follow up later.

Leaving is always a tricky thing for people to do correctly. Since we, as introverts, don't need a whole lot of attention, leaving can be awkward. When it's time to leave, I just want to leave, so I get up and do it.

AFTER THE EVENT

Okay. Very important is what to do after the event. The event is over, and you made it home.

If it was a more personal event, so not like an event at a luxury car dealership or something like that, but more of a personal event where you got an actual invite from a person or there's some kind of definite leader or organizer of this event, you are going to need to send a handwritten thank-you note.

Mail it. Mail a handwritten thank-you note. You can also send an email saying, "Hey, thanks. It was a great time. I learned XYZ." But in addition to that, you need to send a handwritten thank-you note, thanking them for inviting you to the event.

The reason for this is that almost nobody does that, so you will stand out. You will be remembered. So when there's something else, they would be sure to invite you because they remember you, and they remember you appreciated them. Out of whoever showed up, you will most likely be the only one to do that. It'll be noted, and you will be well on your way to excelling in your network. Make sure you do that. It's very important. Easy to do, easy to not do...so do it.

I cannot stress how important this is and the difference it makes.

SUMMARY

Hey, it's time for a review.

So, what did we learn? Don't ask, "What do you do?"

Don't do it.

You'll be invisible. You don't want to be invisible. You want to be *seen*. You want to be noted and remembered.

So instead you might want to say, "What project are you

working on? What's something interesting that happened this week to you? Ask something like that but never ask, "What do you do?" You're going to find out what they do. It will come up, but don't ask. Don't ask it. Don't do it.

Don't act rich, important, or smart unless you are. And even if you are, then still don't act that way, because people don't tend to respond well to that pompousness. They'll know. They'll know. They'll notice if you're smart. You don't have to act smart. The people will pick up the fact that you're pretty bright. Or, if you're rich, they'll figure it out. Or, if you're important, they'll figure that out over time, too, but you don't have to push that on them.

So, if you are genuinely a big deal, you don't have to be like, "Hey, look at me!" And if you aren't, you don't have to pretend to be that way, because they'll find out. And it's not going to end well for your efforts of trying to build something real with these people.

Be an active listener. Remember, listen like you are about to learn something that's going to be useful to you and like they have something important to say. People are very fascinating if you actually listen to them. You know most of the time people don't really listen to you, and how great it would be if someone really truly listened to what you were saying. And so, do that for somebody else. Actually listen to them. Don't cut them off, just let them vent, express, say whatever they want to say. Listen and then follow up.

Take it easy on using people's names. Yes, it's good to use and remember names, but don't overdo it.

Share your interests. Remember, if you are interested in something or you have hobbies, let people know what your hobbies are. "I enjoy XYZ. I'm fascinated by ABC." Like for me, sailboats. I love sailboats.

I want to go hot-air ballooning, too—I have never done that. There's some stuff that I'd like to do, and there's some stuff that I have done that I am very passionate about, and I'd like to do more of, like sailing. But you have to let people know your interests, and you might bond over it.

I like scotch and cigars. And when I bring up, "Hey, I like scotch and cigars," sometimes I meet other people who like scotch and cigars. Then we have something to talk about, and I can invite them to have scotch and cigars somewhere. I often get invited to have scotch and cigars by other people, so it really broadens things and helps you out if people know what you're into. So, share your interests.

Help struggling people. Like my story of the husband and wife who brought their baby to the wine festival. They were definitely struggling, and I thought, *It looks like they could use a friend. I'm going to go over there.*

So, if you see a situation where you're out at any sort of social event and it seems like someone could use a hand, or a friend, or something, go over there and introduce yourself.

There's no guarantee they are going to be cool and that it's going to end up being a great lasting friendship. But it's the right thing to do, and this policy has served me very well. I think that everyone can really benefit from it. You never know who's watching. Somebody else can see that you're actually cool helping people. However, you're not doing it for the image. You're doing it because you know sometimes people need help or a friend. You'll definitely learn from it, and it will take you places you never dreamed and make you a better person.

By networking at events, you'll have enhanced dating opportunities if that is what you're looking for. It will be much more natural than almost any other way. So, if that's what you are looking for, you'll find it.

Network with students. Remember, students grow up to be real adult humans later on, so it's really cool. They'll have a lot of questions, and if you are in a position that you have the experience that will allow you to answer some of their questions, that's great!

They get a lot of value out of it, and you get value too because they say when you teach someone something, you learn it over again. You get different perspectives from what questions are asked of you, and you might get a fresh view on the subject. It might help you out. So, there's a lot you can learn from students, and they can learn from you. Then, they grow up to be whatever, and you know people who do whatever it is they grow up to do. So, if you can, do it.

Don't kiss ass. These are your peers. When you show up to some kind of event, don't be kissing people's asses. You're all there for a reason. You're all on the list. You've all been invited so act like you belong there. This is your spot. You're there just like everybody else, so talk to people like they're at your level. Don't talk down to anyone and don't do the "I'm your biggest fan!" sort of thing.

The thank-you card: if an actual person invited you to something and you go, you need to follow up with a handwritten thank-you card. It will definitely set you apart because pretty much nobody else is doing that. You will be remembered and most likely invited again to other things—plus, it's just a really nice thing to do. I know I like getting thank-you cards. And it is very rare that I get one. But I absolutely give them, and it makes a huge difference in how people follow up with you and their impressions of you. You get access to a lot more opportunities when people know you actually appreciated what they did. So...handwritten thank-you cards.

Got it? Good. Let's keep moving forward.

Chapter Five

CONNECTING WITH A HEADLINER/VIP

At some events you attend, there might be a main headliner. Sometimes there isn't, and it's just a gathering of people.

However, if there is a headliner or VIP at the event and you want to meet that person, how do you do that?

For us introverts, it's a little different. We have different ways of doing things that might be better for us and more comfortable. So, we're going to get into how you would go about doing that, what's worked for me, and I'll give you some examples as well. It's going to be fun!

ACCESS THE HEADLINER OR VIP

Okay. So, here's what most people do if there is a headliner they want to meet. The VIP comes down from the stage during a break and says something like, "I'll be around during the break. You can ask me questions and talk to me."

And when they come down from the stage, the average person joins the mob of people who gathers around the VIP trying to get some personal attention. We introverts think, *I'd like to meet them, too, but how am I supposed to go talk to that person when there's a mob of people around them?*

Being introverted and shy, I can't just elbow my way through and yell out my question, and even if I could, it's not going to make a really good impression.

So, what are we supposed to do? Before I knew what to do, I spent a lot of time waiting on the side hoping maybe everyone will ask their questions, disperse, and then I could get in there. But what happens is there's someone who hogs all the time and then the break is over, and you never get to talk to that person or meet them.

So, what do you do? Here is what has worked for me.

I will observe. Remember I said to get to the event early. If you arrive early, usually you'll see the headliner wandering around a little bit with some other people. Notice who they are with.

Usually there is someone who has unlimited and immediate access to the headliner. This person might be their personal assistant or their friend.

There's usually a small entourage, maybe one, two, or three people who are with the headliner who seem to have access to that person. And whenever those people are around, they are able to immediately get the attention of and talk to the VIP, so you need to take a mental note of who these people are. When that break time happens, instead of trying to go through the mob and talk to the headliner, go introduce yourself to one of those people—the assistant or the friend of the headliner.

Usually, they are available. During the break there might be two of them just standing there talking to each other and a third one doing something else. Usually there is no demand to talk to them because they're not the headliner. They're just someone who the headliner knows. And so what I'll do is go up and introduce myself, talk to them, open them with a light conversation, and I might mention, "I would really like to meet the headliner, but you know I'm really shy and you see that mob. How would that possibly happen?"

If you've made a good impression on this person who knows the headliner, they will say, "Oh, I'll hook you up."

And they will arrange for you to meet the headliner. That's

happened to me several times, and it's worked out really well.

Remember, this person is the friend or assistant to the headliner, and they will be vetting you. If they think the headliner would be annoyed by meeting you, they will not provide the introduction. The introduction will only be provided if they think the headliner would actually enjoy meeting you.

An interesting twist for me is, even though my goal was to meet the headliner, I end up finding out that most of the time, the person I end up liking most and become friends with is the friend or personal assistant of the headliner. They end up being the person who becomes an important part of my network, the person who I really enjoyed being around.

Yes, I meet the headliners, and they're fine too, but they're usually a little different than I imagined they'd be. I have bonded with headliners as well, but more often than not, it's their friend or assistant that I make the strongest connection with.

I have experiences on the other side of that as well. I have a friend or two who are headliners in certain fields, and I have access to them. I hang out with them in our private lives all the time. And so, at their events I'll make my way around the audience, and people will be like, "How do I meet that person?"

If I think they're cool, I'll grab my friend (the VIP/headliner) and bring him over to meet them. I can just be like, "Hey, meet so-and-so…" Or, sometimes I tell my friend, the headliner, "Hey, you have to meet this one guy (or girl). They're really cool."

And my friend will listen to me because he knows if I say they should meet someone, they probably ought to meet them. They trust my judgment, so it works both ways.

A COUPLE OF EXAMPLES

There was an event I went to where the headliner said, "I'm going to be hanging out at this bar." I think there were maybe thirty people who showed up. So, everyone gathered around. I showed up early, and I watched the headliner come in with two people.

The headliner talked, and everyone gathered around. I was sitting at the bar, and one of the friends of the headliner came over to the bar to get his drink and to talk to the bartender. He was standing next to me.

While he was waiting for the bartender to get his drink, I talked to him. We started a conversation, and we hit it off pretty well. He then asked me if I had met the headliner, and I said, "No. I'd like to. But I'm not going to battle this crowd." And he said, "Oh, no problem. I think he would like to meet you." And then he walked into the crowd, grabbed the headliner, brought him over to me, and said, "Meet Nick." And I had a good four- or five-minute conversation with him.

We had our three, our group of three, the headliner, the headliner's friend, and me.

Everybody else was just standing around talking to each other and waiting. After a few minutes, the headliner got back to talking with everyone else and all that, but I got a nice chunk of time with him. It was great. And still to this day, I know the headliner, and I'm friends with the friend of the headliner.

Another example: I was invited to go to a cigar bar. I like cigars and have a friend who likes cigars, and he said, "Meet me at the cigar bar. They have a live jazz band on this particular evening, and it's going to be a great time."

I showed up, sat at the bar, which I hate doing because being a bit of a shy guy, I know when you sit at the bar, you usually have to talk to people. I didn't feel like talking to people that evening, but it was the only place available to sit.

I sat at the bar and made sure there was an extra barstool for my buddy when he got there.

I ordered a drink and waited. After a few minutes, he texted and said, "I'm not going to make it." So, I was thinking, *Maybe I should just leave.*

The band was really good. They were playing Brazilian jazz. I love Brazilian jazz. It was great! So, I decided, *Well, I'll hang out here for a while and look around, see what I want to do.*

Then I realized, *I know what to do. I know what to do here.*

I looked around, took in the atmosphere and used my observation skills. I saw there was a stunningly beautiful girl sitting in the far corner and thought, *If I wasn't shy and introverted, I would talk to her. She is absolutely stunning, and I'd like to hear what her story is, but for now, I'm just going to sit right here at this bar while I figure this whole thing out.*

The bartender was checking up on everybody. When he came by, I said, "How are your martinis?"

He said, "Well, they're pretty good."

A little side note here...I like to consider myself a connoisseur of gin martinis. I make a lot of them myself, and I judge other people's martinis pretty harshly.

I told him, "I'm really particular about mine, but I'd like you to make me one, and let's see how you do."

He replied, "Challenge accepted. Let's give it a shot!" He made a martini, handed it to me, stood by while I took a sip, and said, "Let me know. Let me know." And it was actually really good!

So, I told him, "You did a really good job. Well done!"

He was very happy. I was happy. And he went off to take care of some other customers. I listened to a few songs, then he came back.

I told him, "I really like this venue. I like the layout. I like how it's all set up. I like the band. You did a really great job here in the way this was all put together."

He said, "Thank you very much. I appreciate it."

I told him how great the drinks were because they *were* great. So, I wasn't making anything up. This was really nice.

It was about that time the owner walked in, and the bartender pointed him out to me and said, "The owner is here."

"Oh, man, that's cool. I'd like to tell him how I like this place, but you know…"

And he said, "Well, you can."

"Well, I'm not going to…I'm sure he's busy and he has stuff to do. He can't be bothered with me."

"No. I'll bring him over."

So, he brought the owner over, and I said, "I really like what you did here. The bartender is awesome. He's really been on top of his game. I like how you laid out the place, love the band. You've done great things here. I'm going to tell my friends about this place."

He was very happy with that. Now about this time, the band was going on break. They came over to talk to the owner, and the owner introduced me to the band. "Hey, this is Nick."

And so, I met the band.

So, the band is standing with me having a couple of drinks, and the owner is standing on the other side of me talking. I knew what my next move was. I looked over at the beautiful girl in the corner and kept looking until she made eye contact. Then I waved her over because I had the owner and the band here, so the chances were pretty high she'd come over, right?

She did. She got up and came over because, hey, if there's some guy that's talking to the...I don't know if she knew that was the owner or not, but she knew that was the band and they were hanging out with me. So, I guess she felt, *Well, let's see what's going on.* So, she came over, and I introduced myself, the owner, and the band. It was really smooth and really easy because I'm set up and settled in. She's coming over to my space. I wasn't going over to hers.

We had a nice conversation. Great, great woman. I found out she was a professional ballerina and was in town doing a show, a performance. So, we all talked for quite some time. The band went back and played some more, and I talked with that beautiful girl, the owner, and the bartender.

Long story short, the band invited me to come be their guest at another one of their shows happening the following week. The ballerina girl gave me tickets to come see her at one of her performances. And the owner and bartender invited me to come back again. So, it was a really great night, a *really* great night. That's what happens if you pay attention, listen, and use these techniques.

Now, there wasn't necessarily a headliner, but I did want to meet the band and that girl. It all started with the bartender, then the owner, then the band, then the girl, and it all came together. Don't underestimate these techniques I'm explaining to you. Everything has a domino effect and can build on the previous step. Put these skills to use, and you'll be surprised what you can do.

SUMMARY

Time for our review.

In order to meet a VIP, headliner, or specific person, you are going to want to observe.

Observe who they came in with, who they're with, who has access to them. There's always somebody around who has access to them.

Then connect with one of the people who has access to the person. Go up, introduce yourself, and talk to them as I have explained. Once you have established the basic connection, you're going to express your intent. You're going to let them know, "I would really like to meet that person. It'd be cool to meet that person." And they (if you did it right) will help you meet that person because it's easy for them to do.

I'm not saying it's always going to work, but this is way easier to do than battling the mob. It's easier just to be a friend of a friend. So, give it a try, apply it, and I think you'll be pleased with the results. It's worked great for me. I think it'll work wonderfully for you.

Chapter Six

NETWORKING IN THE WORKPLACE

Networking in the workplace can be very valuable. You spend a lot of time there. You have to be there anyway, so you might as well make the best of the situation, right? You know being known at work really helps to further your career, get things done, and makes it an overall more pleasant place to be.

Also, not just networking in your immediate workplace, but networking in the industry or in industries that are complementary to yours is also very helpful. So, we're going to go over some things that will help you excel in networking in your workplace and industry.

WORKPLACE EVENTS

First things first. There's always going to be some kind of company function like a holiday party, a summer picnic, team-building exercises, or sometimes there will be volunteer opportunities where a group of company people go and volunteer to work at the soup kitchen or something like that. Go to all of these things. Go to as many as you can because it will really enhance your networking and you'll be able to use some of the techniques you've learned in these situations. Plus, it's a really good opportunity to meet some new people.

AT THE EVENT

Let's say you're at a company function and there's alcohol there. Don't get drunk. You can have a drink; you can have two. Don't get completely trashed. I see it all the time. I go to these functions, and there's always somebody who does it. Don't let that be you. It does not help your cause to be completely wasted at a company function.

If you have a spouse or significant other, try to rein them in and not have them get completely trashed either, because that reflects on you as well. So, you're just going to be there, be sociable, but don't get all out of control. You want to be able to maintain your composure. You're going to use a lot of the same techniques as before, like the Cape Walk and the duke/duchess cookie face.

You should know some people already because you work with them. These are your coworkers, so you should automatically have some people you can go up and talk to because you see them every day. You can start with people you know, have your group of three, and then you can break off from there, introvert hunting. Maybe there are some people you don't know, and they might be around the fringes with their cell phones out. Go get 'em!

Also, if there's somebody you have only met briefly, this is your time to expand learning more about them and bring them into the fold. So, if you have your group of two, you can bring one of those people in and work the Magic of Three. You're going to use all the basics we learned before in this, plus we have some specific things to talk about that apply to the workplace.

WHAT TO TALK ABOUT

Right out of the gate, I have to tell you to do something that might not seem to make sense.

I'm going to ask you to not talk about work. Sure, at work you will have to talk about work, but when you are networking and socializing at work, don't talk about work.

It's similar to what I've told you before with other social events. I said, *Don't ask people what they do.*

At work, workplace events, you probably know what people do, or maybe you don't, but still don't talk about work. Why? Because everybody *always* talks about work. They start off talking about work, and most people don't want to talk about work. They want to talk about their interests.

So, you're going to say stuff like, "What project do you have coming up?" Not necessarily work projects. "What are you doing this holiday weekend? What's going on?" You're going to try to reach in and get to whatever their interests are, whatever their hobbies outside of the workplace are, because they're going to be more interested in talking about that most likely.

Depending on the workplace, for some people, their work is also their hobby—like if you're into computer programming or something like that, and that's also your job and you're really into it, then maybe they want to talk about that. And if you want to talk about that, then by all means talk about it, but you can start off saying, "What are you doing this holiday weekend?"

And if they say, "I'm going to be working on this computer program," and that is something you also want to talk about, then go ahead and engage because they're apparently passionate about it.

Usually I find that people don't necessarily want to talk

about work. They want to bond over other topics. A popular topic a lot of people default to is gossip. I recommend you stay away from that. Gossip has a way of making its way back around and ending badly, so it's best to avoid it.

Instead, talk about interests.

I've been able to talk about whiskey, cigars, sailboats, deep sea fishing, and travel.

There are all kinds of topics, and everyone has something they would love to discuss. I know several people who are beekeepers. I bring that up a lot, beekeeping, and I've asked enough questions that now I can compare and say, "So-and-so is a beekeeper. They said that this XYZ makes their bees ABC...Do you find it to be the same way with your bees?"

There are all kinds of topics you can talk about, but you're going to want to steer away from work if you can. The way to build connections with people in the workplace, believe it or not, is by not talking about work. It's by talking about interests. And their interest might not be the same as yours. In fact, most of the time it won't be, but you can always learn something new.

Find something out that's interesting about their interest because you can always learn. People are fascinating if you're listening, so be an active listener like we talked about before, and listen like it's something important. Listen like you're about to learn something and give them your attention.

WHAT TO TALK ABOUT #2

Once again, just as before, do not kiss ass. Don't go around the workplace kissing people's asses; just be a human being talking to another human being.

So even if your position is kind of lofty or it's in the middle, don't wipe your ass with these people. Actually, treat them with respect and kindness because it's the right thing to do, and it will pay off in ways you can't even begin to imagine.

This isn't just talking to the senior people in your company. You need to talk to everybody. So, whether it be the person who's taking out the trash, the mailroom person, or if it's the vice president of the company, you treat everybody with the same level of respect. It's served me well. And for everybody who has used these networking techniques, it has served them well also.

Remember these are your peers. Regardless of your title, you're all at the same level. You're talking to them, you see them, you give them a voice.

Bridging the rank gap is also much easier if you don't talk about work. Because if you talk about work, then you're like, "Well, you're making decisions here and I'm here," or, "You're taking out the trash and I'm here."

Now if you talk about your hobbies, then you're all just people who have interests. So that's another important point to think about.

Another note about talking to everyone. I make it a point to speak and treat with respect all of the maintenance people, the security guards, contractors, and everyone, because you never know who you are going to meet. A lot of these folks are really good people, and as I mentioned before, you don't know who these people know. You might be on vacation and think, *This hotel maid can't do anything for me but clean my room and get out of the way.* However, I always make time to engage and speak with the cleaning staff of the hotels I stay in because they almost always have cool and interesting stories to share, and I've gotten really outstanding recommendations about restaurants, salsa clubs, and, in general, things to do or see in that city.

I've been invited to people's homes for dinner and also fishing trips. Once again, you never know who you are going to meet and what fascinating things you can learn or experience, but you have to be open to talking to people from all ranks and positions.

OPENERS (THINGS TO SAY)

So, you say, "Nick, when I'm first engaging people, what do I say there? Just give me a few things to say."

So, here's some stuff you can say.

"Hi. I'm Nick." But you would say your name, obviously. It doesn't have to be some kind of code or cryptic thing, just "Hi. I'm Nick." That simple. Walk up and say that.

Another popular one: "I don't think I've met you yet."

One of my favorites: "I came to shake some hands! I'm Nick."

This one works too: "I like your ___, where did you get it?"

Need some more?

"What brings you here tonight?"

"What are you hoping to learn tonight?"

"What is that accent you have?"

"How do you know the host?"

If there are some people on the side I want to meet, I can do a sweeping intro. Engage the first person, then say, "Who are your friends?" as I gesture to the nearby people and introduce myself down the line.

There you go. Very simple stuff that you can have in your bank to initially make that first opening volley.

THANKING PEOPLE

Thank people a lot. In your workplace or your industry, if anyone does anything remotely cool, thank them. Thank them for it. Let them know. You can send an email, but it's better in person or through an actual thank-you card. Most of the time, people do not get thanked. In my case, I work with a lot of engineers. I'm known for not really having a lot of love for engineers because engineers tend to make things a lot more difficult than they have to be.

When an engineer actually does something good, it's a big deal, so I make sure to thank them. I will get a thank-you card and write out, "Hey, thank you for XYZ. I really appreciate it." And we have an ice cream place here that's really nice that has gift cards. So, I get a ten-dollar gift card, put it in the thank-you card, and say, "Have a cold one on me."

No one else does this, so when they get it, they're like, "What? Wow!"

My point is, people aren't used to getting thanked, especially a "thanks" like that, so it makes you stand out and they remember you.

Anytime anyone at any position, whether it's the VP of the company or the security guard, does something cool, thank them. You can do it face-to-face, "Thank you. I appreciate this. I want you to know it was noticed that you did this, and I really appreciate it." And actually be grateful to them for that. It really makes an impact on that person, and it helps everybody.

It helps them, it helps you, it makes the workplace a better place, and it helps build relationships where people are not invisible. They know you see them.

Thank people every opportunity you get when they do something that is worthy of being thanked.

It will make a lot of doors open up for you.

In this section I talked a little smack about engineers. It's all in good fun. I am aware that a lot of good things we enjoy in society are the direct result of the efforts of great engineers. Engineers also make up a good percentage of my network as well as a large percentage of women I've dated. So...engineers, I salute you!

MORE WAYS TO CONNECT IN THE WORKPLACE

Here are more examples of things you can talk about. There is a coworker who had a child; well, she has two children and they're around the same ages as some of my nieces and nephews. So, I said to her, "My nephew's birthday is coming up, and he's around the same age as your son. I want to get a gift. I want to win the gift giving. I want to be the one who gives the best gift for his birthday. What's the hot toy? What is the gift that will beat everyone else in gift giving for this kid?"

And so, what happens is—she's happy to help. She's like, "Oh, yeah, so this is the latest," because I know she knows. I don't have kids. I'm not in that sphere, but I know that since she has kids, she'll know.

And so, she says, "Oh, this is the latest hot toy out. This is what everybody wants."

And I say, "Hey, thank you." And then I actually go get that for my nephew.

And then what happens is...now I've built this little relationship.

I didn't just come up and ask about some work report or something. I asked her opinion, came to her for her to consult with me on what is the best gift.

She gave her opinion on what that is. Now, when she sees me if I don't see her first, she's going to say, "Hi. How did it go?" She will wonder how it went. She'll wonder if I followed her advice and got the toy, and if I was successful in winning the gift giving. A victory for me is a victory for her.

She knows I came to her. I could have gone and asked advice from anyone, but I came to HER. And so, when I see her, I'll say, "Hey! That really worked out. That was awesome! Thank you. I won!" or I can say, "Wow! That was a horrible gift idea. I was beaten by this other person who gave this other gift, and now I know that your advice for gift giving sucks. You're not the one to come to." Then we can laugh about it.

I'm not saying to actually yell at her. No. You can joke with her about how "that wasn't really good," or, "Oh, man. It was awesome." It's about reassurance and relationship building.

The next time you see them, if they gave you a bad gift idea, you can be like, "My anniversary is coming up. You got any bad gift ideas for me?"

Or if they do give good advice, you can hit them up about whatever because you've opened up that door. You've established this relationship. It's not based on "work stuff" like "Did you get that work report in?" or something like that. It's an outside thing.

That has served me really well: asking people's advice about giving a gift to somebody or different activities that I might like. I could say, "My anniversary is coming up, and I want to take my lady someplace nice. What do you think would be a good place to take her? I don't want it to be too over the top but I want it to be special. Do you have any suggestions? What do you think would be a good spot?"

This could be that same person, or it could be a different person. They would give you their two cents, and you might use their advice or not. So, you could either come back and say, "Oh, no. I found out she would prefer this other place, so I took her there," or you could say, "Yeah, I took her to your spot."

And so once again, you're establishing this. You know you're trusting them with "I came to you. You gave me this advice and..." They are going to be curious about how their advice worked out for you.

In your workplace, you are establishing these little relationships on the side. Then whenever you see them, they'll be like, "Oh. That's Nick. He comes to me for his advice on where to take his dates," or, "He comes to me for his advice on gift buying."

So, you establish these little relationships, and they grow more and more over time.

Another example is with one of our company vice presidents. I was in a meeting with him, and after the meeting I said, "Can I have a word with you really quick? It's not about work."

And he's like, *Oh, I wonder what this is about.*

And I said, "So I went on this date the other night, and I think I messed it up. But I want to walk you through what I did and see if you can point out the spot where I messed up. Man to man, I need your insight on this."

And he said, "Oh. Yeah! Let me hear about this." It had nothing to do with work, but he was curious because people love to hear about stuff like that and weigh in on it.

So, then I walked him through my date, and he gave his feedback. The next time I saw him when I walked into a meeting he was like, "Nick, how are things!? Let's catch up after the meeting!" and everyone else was thinking, *What? How is...how do these guys know each other? How is Nick all chummy with the VP?*

Simple, the VP wants to be updated about my dates and if I took any of his advice.

**It has been my experience that most senior executives of corporations give pretty bad dating advice. Just FYI.

Once again, you need to keep your eyes open, observe, and ask. You can either ask for advice about something, or you can just inquire if you find out they have a hobby that's interesting. You can ask, "What are the challenges in that hobby? What have you accomplished in that hobby?"

I think it's fascinating, especially because you can see them get really excited when talking about it. And I think we all win because I learn something, and they get to shine in expressing and explaining their passion. When I meet someone else with a similar hobby, I have some familiarity with it. It's just finding different ways by observing. You can always connect by asking people questions or their advice on something.

A lot of times, the best technique for networking in the workplace is by asking advice. People do this to me as well. They'll come by and say, "So this is what happened. What do you think I should do in this scenario?" And then I say my thing, "This is what I think you should do." And then when I see them, I say, "Did you do it? What happened?" So, it works both ways.

But once again, peers, you talk like this with the person who takes out the trash. You talk like this with the vice president of the company. It's all the way around; you're humans. Everyone has things they're interested in, passionate about, or could use advice on, or they want to help you with something. So, don't be afraid to say, "I need your help on this."

And if it's not about work, then usually they're like, "Oh. Yeah." If it's something that they're interested in, they will be more than happy to give you their advice, and then they will follow up with you on how their advice went because they're really curious.

These techniques allowed me to build a very strong network through all levels of my workplace as well as with people in the industry. This allowed me to have many opportunities for advancement as well as job offers from other companies in the industry. It can do the same for you. So, take this advice, use it, and get back to me. Let me know how it worked out for you.

NEW HIRES

New people. New people are great because they're not comfortable yet and don't know anybody. So, if you're at a company and they hire someone new, whether it's an individual or a group, make sure you go and meet these people immediately.

What I like to do if it's a new group of people is I will talk to whoever's running that group and say, "Give me ten minutes to talk to them." I go in, introduce myself, and say, "If you see me around, come up and say hi. If you need anything or have any questions, please use me as a resource." And I'll meet all of them, shake their hands, and hear a little bit about each one.

Yes, I'm shy and introverted, but at the same time, they have to be a little more reserved than me because they're new. They don't know what's going on. I've been there for a long time, so I can meet these people on my terms.

It could be six months later. "Hey, Nick, what's going on?"

And I say, "Oh, hey."

They remember me as one of the first people they met when they started working there.

If it's an individual who just started, let's say a new engineer or something like that, I go up, introduce myself, and say, "I just wanted to introduce myself and welcome you on board. And if you need anything, if I can answer any questions or be of any sort of help or assistance to add value in any way, please let me know."

And for their desk, I might get them a Rubik's Cube or something. "Here's a Rubik's Cube for your desk so you have a desk toy."

I try to welcome people with a desk toy of some sort, like the Magic 8-Ball that makes the decisions or a Rubik's Cube or something like that, so they have their first desk decoration and they'll feel welcomed. Then when I'm making my rounds, I'll go and check up on them. "How are you getting settled in? Everybody treating you well? Do you have any questions yet?"

This way, once again, I'm one of the first people they met, and they're like, "Oh, that's Nick. When I first got here, he came by. He gave me this Rubik's Cube, and he welcomed me on." Then later, as they progress and meet more people, their network is expanding, and my network is expanding. So, when I go to a company function, they might introduce me to a whole bunch of people they've met in their section of the workplace that I wouldn't have normally had the opportunity to meet.

And vice versa, I can say, "Come over and meet these people." And so, it just builds that way. It's a great way to add on to your network and know more people. It's getting them fresh when they're new. In the company you work for, make sure no matter what level they're at—no matter if it's a new person working in the mailroom, if it's a new executive, or if it's just a new middle management person or wherever they are—be sure to go out of your way to go introduce yourself and meet them.

Even if your departments don't work together, intersect, or

intertwine, go meet them anyway, because it doesn't hurt to meet new people and to be one of the first people they meet in the workplace. It helps you, and it helps them.

CUSTOM EVENTS AND SHARED EXPERIENCES

Making events at work. So, I told you about attending work events, but one of the most fun things is to make your own work event.

Here's an example of that. I had never really had caviar before. I might have had it, but I didn't remember, so I decided to have a caviar event at work.

I went to a store that sells that sort of thing and got several different types of caviar with all the accoutrements, all the crackers, and everything that goes with it, and I took it to one of the break rooms. I then invited everyone who was at the workplace that day (it was on a weekend, so it was significantly fewer people than if it would have been during the week). "I'm having a caviar tasting event today around lunchtime. Swing by the main break room."

And I explained, "I don't know anything about caviar. I don't know if I like it or don't like it, but we have several different types and we're going to try it out. We're going to go down the line and we're going to try each one and discuss it, and we're going to learn. So, if you want to give it a shot, come on by. If you've never had it or you've had it and like it, come on by and try some of my unique team building."

And it was a good turnout. We had caviar that day, and I found out that I'm not a fan, not a fan of caviar. Am I on a list for caviar? Yes. I added my name and email to all the caviar lists I could find. I do not care for caviar. I learned that at the workplace and shared the experience. I strongly advise you to be a part of people's firsts. Be a positive part of an experience people have that they'll remember.

So now, everyone who was there who had never had caviar before, anytime they see caviar or hear about caviar, they will think of their experience at my event. "Oh, Nick had a caviar event...I tried it at Nick's thing. I had four different types, and I found out that I really like it," or, "I found out that I don't like it. And we had a really good time that day."

I wasn't just going to buy a bunch of caviar and sit in my apartment and eat it alone in the dark.

No, I figured other people probably are in the same boat and they're curious about it, too. Let's all have this together.

You can do this, too. Nothing stops you from having little events of your own and bringing people in to share the moment. A lot of great relationships are formed by having a shared moment like that, a shared experience, a first-time experience. And if you can be someone's first-time experience, it has a really good impact on them and helps strengthen your relationship because you had that experience together. So, I highly advise you to give it a try.

Another example that's not in the workplace is when I chartered my first yacht.

I said, "Let's get some people together, some of my friends and some strangers, some people from the mall, and get them out on the yacht, too." I had never been on a yacht before. But I thought, *I'm going to go out, other people would probably want to go out on a yacht, so I'll invite some people and we're going to experience this together. We're all going to share our first yacht experience.*

Everyone who went on the yacht that day, they all remember. We all bonded over our first yacht experience. It was outstanding, and people came up to me and said, "I never thought I would ever be able to have this experience. Thank you very much."

"You're welcome. Me too, we're doing this! We're having this experience together."

And so now, whenever I think about yachts, see a yacht, or whenever I go on another yacht, I always think back to that first experience when we went out. And I know the same happens with those people. Whenever they see a yacht or hear about a yacht, they'll think, *Oh man! Nick took me out for my first yacht experience!*

Sure, they might have other yacht experiences, but they'll always remember the first, and I got to help make that experience special. That has a huge impact on people when you can be a part of their firsts. You can do it in the workplace like with the caviar event, or you can do it outside of the workplace. Just think of something you want to experience, and simply include others in that experience as well.

Like with the helicopter—I had never been on a helicopter before. I chartered the helicopter, got my cousin, and said, "You're going to experience this, too. Get in." And so now, he's been on other helicopters since then, but he'll always remember the first, and that was with me.

So be a part of people's firsts if you can. If you are going to experience something and you have the opportunity to share that experience with other people, do it. It really forms strong bonds. That is a very important takeaway. Be part of people's firsts. Share the experience.

SUMMARY

Let's review networking in the workplace and in the industry.

There are always events happening; there's always going to be some side stuff outside of the workplace—team building, volunteering, the summer party, or holiday party. Go. Go. Go. Even if you don't want to go, still go. Most of the time, I don't want to go, but I go. You have to go because this is what makes the whole thing work—you have to show up.

When you're there, don't talk about work. Unless you are directly working on a project, then it's fine. But when you're making your rounds and socializing, don't talk about work, because everyone talks about work. It makes you invisible. You want to stand out. You want to talk about their interests and to talk about advice, but don't talk about work.

Treat everyone with respect. From the highest of the high to the lowest of the low and everywhere in between in the hierarchy of the workplace, treat everyone with respect. Don't be like, "Well, I'm up here, so I'm looking down on you." And then if someone's up there, don't be thinking, *Oh, you're so great!* and kissing their ass. You treat everyone with respect. Don't kiss ass and don't wipe your ass with anybody. These are your peers.

Thank people. When somebody does something that is

worthy of thanking, don't just assume they know you're thankful. No. You actually need to tell them, and it's great if it's face-to-face. Shake their hand, look at them, and say, "Thank you. I appreciate it." And/or send an actual thank-you card, a handwritten thank-you card that says, "Thank you. I appreciate this." You can send an email too, but the handwritten thank-you card is absolutely way better than an email.

Ask for advice and ask about their interests. "My cousin is turning seven, and you have a seven-year-old or an eight-year-old. What do you think I should get? I think you would probably know about that," or, "Do you have any advice?" or, "I'm going on a third date, and I don't know..." "Well, she said she likes miniature golf, but I don't..." "Do you know anything about..." "Is there a good place, a better place than...?"

There are a lot of different things we can ask people's advice about and then ask about their interests. "I saw you riding that bicycle, and you seem really competitive. Have you won any competitions doing that? What's the crowd turn-out like? Do they have corndogs there or snacks for people who show up to watch? Do people throw Gatorade on you?"

"How much does your bike weigh? I hear that the weight is important."

"Do you shave your legs like swimmers?"

The point is there are all kinds of different questions you can ask when you're learning about people's interests.

New people. When anyone is new in the workplace, it's the best time because they're not settled in. They're shaky. They don't know who you are or how you fit into the hierarchy yet. It's a perfect time to show up, introduce yourself, say, "How can I help? If I can help, feel free to reach out." And they will remember you because you're one of the first people they met and you were nice to them. Or you can go and be mean, I guess. They'll remember that, too.

Go get those new people, it's a great way to expand your network.

You can make events. So, like me with the caviar event, I thought it would be a cool thing to do. We bonded over the caviar that day, and it was great!

We also did a chili competition and a clam chowder competition a few months later with good success.

These things help bring people together and help bond you in the workplace and industry. If you can, invite some people from outside the industry, or if you're attending events like these and meeting people in complementary industries, that's great, too.

Chapter Seven

FOLLOW-UP EVENTS

This is a great one. Once you get in the habit of attending events, usually there'll be a follow-up event and you may get an invite. So if you've done what you're supposed to do, if you made some connections, got in good with the host, sent a handwritten thank-you letter after an event, chances are you will get invited to another event.

If you get invited to a follow-up event, once again, you need to go. It's a really great opportunity to meet some new people and to strengthen the connections you made at the last event. Let's discuss that next, shall we?

PLUS-ONE?

Okay, let's say you made a solid connection at a private museum exhibit, and you look in your mailbox one day and see an invite for an exclusive art event.

You now have some options. You can show up alone, or you can reach out to that one connection you made and say, "Hey, Earl, are you going to the art event?" And he might say, "Oh, I was unaware of the art event." And since usually you'll have a plus-one option, you can bring somebody. You say, "You want to be my plus-one? Just meet me out front at...Here's the date and time if you can."

Now, you're showing up as a pair. You have your pair, and now you just need to get your third while you're in there, but you're showing up from a position of power because you've shown up with someone you know who might have subject-matter knowledge. They also might end up knowing some of the people at this new event because a lot of these events overlap. However, if he can't make it, you simply show up by yourself, and you do the same techniques as before.

When you go in, you're going to be scanning, and you're going to look to see if there is somebody you recognize from the last event. It happens to me; people might recognize me and say, "Oh. Hey, Nick!" And I say, "Hey." And then try to remember their name. Sometimes I remember, sometimes I don't. I admit it if I don't, and they tell me again and I make a mental note to remember.

So, you're going to try to bring someone to the follow-up event if you can. If not, then you're going to look for people who are familiar to you from the previous event. But keep the basics the same and do the cookie face, Cape Walk, go for the food when you get in there, and scan the edges. But first, you're going to look to see if you know anybody.

BUILDING MOMENTUM

The follow-up events are great because they build momentum. So, as you do these events, especially in high-end settings, you're going to notice a lot of the same people go to these. So, if it's polo, most of the same people are going to be there. If it's cars, it's going to be most of the same people. Whatever the category, any other event in that category is going to have a lot of overlap of the same people.

So, when you go to these events, once you start making some key connections, you will see a lot of these people repeatedly, and it snowballs. You meet whoever they're with, they introduce you and you introduce them, and it branches out. It's really great!

Also, when you're at this level, it's a good time to think about making your own event.

For example, I have a sports car, and I enjoy the occasional street race. I know some other people with sports cars and say, "Let's get together and run the cars. Whoever you know who would like to come, bring them too, and let's have some fun on Saturday."

Then you and the guys meet up and run those cars. During this process, you would have met some new people and bonded over the event.

Never underestimate the power of these little events.

*I do not endorse or engage in illegal street racing.

THE WALKTHROUGH

I love this, love it, love it. So, maybe you have reached the level where you know a lot of people at an event, and let's say you have other things to do. You don't really want to be at an event that evening, but you know you have to show up. You are there on the scene, but you want to go home and be alone because you're an introvert and need to recharge, but you still want to get credit for attending the event. Here's what you do.

I present to you "the walkthrough."

Here's how it works: you meet the host, shake their hand, say, "Thanks for having me," and then you walk through each room that is active, each of the areas of that event, and you make eye contact and wave to all the people you know, but you're walking fast. You're walking with purpose like you're on your way to go do something.

With this technique, you don't necessarily need to go over

to the food as you normally would. You can see what they have just in case there's something you want. Feel free to grab a little sandwich or a drink really quick, and then you point, wave, nod, and walk through the event (two times). So, you walk through each section of whatever this function is, two rounds, but you're walking with purpose, nodding to everybody, and then...you just walk outside and go home.

I've done this several times.

So, you're not networking that night; you're just going because you need to go and you, for some reason or another, had an obligation to be at this function. The thing is, everybody sees you, everyone knows you were there, they see you're in a hurry and you're walking with purpose, so they just figure, *Oh, I'll just catch up with him/ her later*. But then, they get distracted, and if for some reason they look for you later, they'll figure you are somewhere around or maybe you had to leave, and they'll just move on.

But they remember you being there. So, when they're talking about the function, they're like, "Oh, yeah, Nick was there. I saw him," and everyone will say, "Yeah, I saw him there. He was there." But you might have been there for maybe ten minutes, and then you were gone. But everyone saw you, so you still get the credit for being there. If it's a function with a dance floor, I'm usually good to grab a gal for one quick dance as well so then people there will remember they saw me on the dance floor.

Keep in mind, this is only good if you already know a lot of people there. And it has to be a large function. If it's a cocktail party at someone's house with just ten people, it's obviously not going to work. It must be a large event, and you must already be known. It's NOT good for you to do this if you're not known. If you are not known, then don't do that. You actually have to go and meet some new people. But if you're known, it's a great, great thing if you need to be there and need to be accounted for but have other things to do. So, that's *the walkthrough*.

SUMMARY

All right, let's review.

Bring a plus-one if you can. By that I mean someone you met at a prior event, if you're going to an event that's similar. For example, if you met and connected with them at a car thing, and you're going to another car thing, reach out and say, "I'm going to this event. Are you going? If you want to, I have a plus-one. You can meet me there." It helps solidify that connection.

You're strengthening that relationship, you're bringing them in, and showing up with someone you know, and you've got the pair, so then you're going to play to get your third in there. But it's a good place to be, and they'll appreciate you inviting them. Who knows? They may invite you to something in the future as well.

Don't invite them with the expectation that they're going to invite you to something in the future. You're simply doing *your* part. Don't "keep score" and think anyone owes you anything just because you invited them somewhere or helped them out. You do your part and bring someone. Help them out and add value to them. It helps you as well because you're showing up with a known someone that you've already bonded with.

Look for people you know. When you're in there, even if you brought the plus-one or if you're by yourself, look for people you may know from a previous event. Because as I said earlier, a lot of the people who attend these events overlap, so if it's a car event or if it's a polo event, a symphony, or something, usually the next event you go to of that type will probably have some of the same people from the previous event because car people go to car events, and symphony people go to symphony events. So, you'll see some overlap.

Look for people you recognize from before. And even if you didn't get a chance to meet them last time but you recognize them, you can say, "I saw you at this other event." And it'll give you a jumping-off point for a conversation.

Continue with the basics. You're still going to have your walk, you're still going to do your Duke Cookie Face, you're still going to go hit the food if there's food and drink, you're still going to scan the edges for the introverts, and still do your magic number of three people when you're socializing. The stuff we learned earlier—that still applies when you're going to these follow-up events.

You can make your own event.

For example, I moved into a luxury apartment building and I wanted to meet my neighbors, so I decided to have a wine and cheese party. I sent out invites to the entire building, and I also sent invites to people I'd met around at other functions who I thought might enjoy wine, cheese, and a little company.

I said, "Everyone is welcome to come over." That way, I can meet my neighbors, have some of my regular friends over, and have some people I met at other functions come by. Although I was still introverted and shy, I put the invite out, had the party, and it turned out great! I got to meet some new people, and because I'm the host, people came to introduce themselves to ME! And whoever they brought, I met those people, too!

So, it's really good to host your own event if you can and invite people that you might have met at some of these other events, like the car event, yachting, polo, or wher-ever. If they have a good time, maybe you'll get invited to one of their events, maybe not. But maybe you will. And this is how relationships form.

The walkthrough: once you are already known by a good deal of people in an event, and if you really need to go but you also need to not be there, the walkthrough is really good. You power your way through, acknowledge every-body, and then you just slip out. But you've been seen, and people just think they lost track of you.

Later on, touch base with the host: "I had to leave early." But still thank them and still send a thank-you card and all that.

Chapter Eight

MAINTAINING RELATIONSHIPS

This is one of the most important chapters if not *the most important*. It's about maintaining your relationships. You start the relationships, develop them, and have these connections in your network. Now, you have to maintain them. If you go through all the trouble of forming these bonds and connections with people and then don't maintain them, it's all gone—it's all a waste. The maintenance is the most important part to keep it all together, so I'm going to show you how to do that now.

KEEPING IN TOUCH

Naturally when keeping in touch, face-to-face is best, but a lot of times you can't do that. Especially if you have an international network, you can't really see everyone face-to-face all the time. But you're going to need to maintain contact with as many people as you can. Now, people fall into different categories—there are really close friends, close friends, friends, colleagues, associates, strong acquaintances, acquaintances, and loose acquaintances.

We're going to focus on strong acquaintances and better.

For everyone else, you see them when you see them unless there is a special exception.

This also doesn't apply to your really close friends, because you'll usually be talking to them all the time anyway.

What you need to do is set a reminder in your calendar, at least quarterly. Every three months or so you need to set aside a week to start going through all of your contacts. Go through your phone, all the phone numbers you have, see who you have in there, and then go through your contacts in your email. See everybody you have in your email, your work, and personal email.

You're going to take a week every three months and go through your phone list, go through your personal email contact list, and go through your work email contact list to see who you have not talked to recently. There are going to be some people you've already talked to and are already up to date with. But for anyone you haven't, make a list of them and work your way down that list. You're going to touch base with each and every person on that list.

There are different ways to do this. You can send something by one of the messengers, like Facebook messenger, WhatsApp messenger, Telegram messenger, or something like that. Hit them up and ask, "What's going on?"

Catch up, get updated.

"How's your kid coming along?"

"How's your engagement?"

"What happened with that cycling race?"

Another option, and one of my personal favorites to do, is to do a video. I realize it's not face-to-face, but I feel it's the next best thing. I'll send a video out so they can see me.

"How are you? What's going on?"

"It's been a little while."

"It's been three months since we talked. What's the latest?"

Touch base with them that way.

You can also make a phone call. Some people, I call. Some people, I send a video. Some people, I'll send an email. Some people, I'll send a written letter through the mail.

It just depends on the relationship with the person and how I feel I want to contact them. But at least quarterly I will reach out to anyone I haven't contacted recently. I make sure to go through my list and hit those people up, contact them, just so I stay fresh in their minds and they stay fresh in mine, so I don't forget them and they don't forget about me.

There will be a lot of people who get lost in the cracks and fade away if you don't stay up on it. I made an effort to meet these people and make them a part of my life. Yes, I am busy, and, yes, I do get sidetracked. But I have to make time to shine a little light and see what they're up to, or see if I can add any value to their lives.

"Can I help you with anything?"

"How are things going?" And touch base with them. You should do the same.

FACE-TO-FACE

Face-to-face is absolutely the best. There is nothing that comes close to it. If you have the means and the time, this is the method you want to use as often as possible. I do a lot of traveling specifically for this purpose. I like to meet with people face-to-face. If you're having a relationship, a friendship, or you're building good strong connections with people, it's best to spend time with them, actually sit down and look at them, and be in their physical presence. This can be an event or having a drink or simply a conversation over a meal. At the end of the day, nothing maintains your relationships better than face-to-face interactions.

People come through Denver, they meet up with me, and we sit down, share a meal, and have good conversation. I do the same with people in other areas of the country and around the world. Those relationships are always a lot stronger than the ones where we don't get the face-to-face time. Try to maintain as many of your relationships through face-to-face contact as possible, and in between those times, send emails, videos, letters, or call.

Face-to-face meetings make all the difference. When someone comes to see you face-to-face, you know how it makes you feel. You know it's the best way. So, you can be the one... Don't say, "Well, they didn't reach out to me."

YOU take responsibility. You do it first. You do it. You step up and do it! And if you keep doing it and they never do it, then maybe you adjust as needed, but you should be the first to step up.

Another thing I would like to add here. You may have heard people say in the past that it is good to live like it's your last day or something like that. What I encourage you to do when you meet with people face-to-face is to treat them like this is the last time you're ever going to see them, like it might be *their* last day. That way you will always treat them with the proper level of respect and connect deeply. And one day, it actually will be the last time you ever see them, and when that day comes, you can rest easy because you were "on the level" the last time you shared a moment with them.

DISCRETION

When you're having these relationships, when you're meeting up with people, bonding, or socializing—let's say you have traveled and met up with someone for drinks or something—a lot of times you're going to learn a LOT about people. They are going to really open up. Especially if you're an active listener, people will share a lot of things with you. So, it's very important to be discreet and not gossip about these people. They are trusting you with certain information. Do not share their sensitive information with other people.

They are confiding in you and similarly you are opening up and being vulnerable to them as well. You need to be someone who is trustworthy. Because if you go and blab and gossip about them, believe me, it's going to get back to them, and it's going to really tarnish that relationship. Look, you wouldn't want anyone doing that to you, so don't do it to them.

If you tell them something in confidence, you want them to keep it between you two.

The same goes the other way. If they feel they can trust you and they let you in on some of their vulnerabilities or something they were concerned about, or they share some things with you, that information doesn't leave the room.

There is a Billy Joel song called "A Matter of Trust." I like that song because it is simple in its message. In ALL relationships, it *always* comes down to a matter of trust. Networking is about relationships with people, and the most important thing in dealing with people is trust.

When you are talking to people, getting to know them, and building relationships, they have to be able to trust you. If they cannot trust you, you're wasting your time. Use discretion when people trust you with something, keep it to yourself, and that's a lesson that will serve you well. *Discretion*. Be worthy of trust. It takes a long time to earn trust, but trust can be lost very quickly. And once it's lost, it is very, very difficult to get back, if ever.

BE HUMBLE AND HONEST

It's cool to meet with people face-to-face and travel, but sometimes you can't. If it's a situation where you want to, but you can't, be sure to let them know.

If for some reason you can't afford to, let them know that too. You don't have to make up an excuse. Just tell them what's up. So, maybe somebody says, "I'm in Switzerland. You should join me, and we can go skiing." And I think, *Man, that's way out of my price range. I can't do that!*

I don't want to say, "Oh, I just...this scheduling, I can't."

No. Instead I would say, "I'd love to do that, but it's out of my price range. I can't afford to do it. I apologize." And simply let them know because it's not as big of a deal as you think it is. But it's messed up if you're trying to say it's something else that it's not. Just tell people the truth.

For example, I was going to Panama and was asking one of my friends to go.

I said, "I'd like you to go to Panama with me."

He said, "Well, my schedule is...I can't really. I don't think I can get the days to go."

And I asked, "Is this about money? Because I want you to

be there. I'll pay. I'll pay for the whole thing. You just need to show up."

"Oh. Yeah, yeah. Okay, I can go."

So, it's best to just be upfront because you never know.

And the same works for other people. If they really want you to come skiing in Switzerland, and you can't afford it, maybe they've got it covered. Maybe they'll take care of it. But you have to tell them, "I can't afford it. It's out of my budget to do that." And then some people will step up. But naturally you can't expect that to happen. You can't expect them to pick up the tab, but I'm just saying, you should let them know. Let people know where you're at. Don't make up bullshit excuses.

Also, if there are high-level events and there's something really out of your price range, don't try to fake like it IS in your price range and like it's some other issue that it's not. Just say what it is, and maybe somebody will step up, maybe they won't. People will appreciate the honesty; I know I do. Be real with it and let them know where you're at.

There's no shame in the game. These are your peers. These are your friends, so be honest and humble, and it will serve you well. No matter what the outcome, you'll be glad you did.

ADDING VALUE

You've heard me say it throughout this book, and I'm sure you hear it many other places these days: ADD VALUE.

Many gurus, mentors, and wise people all tell you to add value when you are interacting with people and networking to strengthen the other person. Always add value.

Then they say, you can't ask the person, "How can I add value to you?" because that is giving the person a task to do. They have to figure out how you can add value, and that apparently is not a cool thing to saddle them with. You are supposed to figure out how to add value to them and simply start doing it.

In some circumstances, this is easy to figure out. For example, I used to be a copywriter. I would write advertising. If I found out someone had a product or a website, I would simply write a few versions of advertising copy for them, assuming I liked their product, and send it over. They wouldn't ask for it. I would just do it, send it over, and say, "If you like any of this, feel free to use it, or not, because I needed to practice my writing anyway." One of the ways I would do that is by picking out products and writing ads about them, so I would simply pick from the products of people I met, write ads about those things, and send it to them. In that way, it was easy to add value to them.

With other people I met, it was much harder. Some people

seem to have pretty much everything covered, and I struggled to come up with a way to contribute or add value to them. So, what did I do?

I can simply be a good friend. I can add value to you by being a good friend. When you call me, I'm there. I listen, give feedback, show up, and support you.

So, if you can't think of anything you can do to add value, you can always just be a good friend. At the end of the day, that's probably the most valuable thing you or I can give to a person.

GIFT GIVING

Giving gifts, in my opinion, is an important part of networking and relationship building. Let me also say that you don't need a reason to give a gift. A lot of people think in order to give a gift it needs to be a holiday, birthday, anniversary, or special occasion.

You can give somebody a gift for no reason at all. You don't have to wait until there is a special day. I believe when you give a gift on a random day, it means *so* much more. It means you were really thinking about the other person. If you give gifts on a holiday or special occasion, a lot of times people are expecting to get something, and I feel that dilutes the actual impact of the gift.

However, if on a random Tuesday, I give you an aloe plant and say, "I was thinking about you and thought you could use an aloe plant," first you might be confused, but then you would most likely be happy that I was thinking about you and your possible aloe plant needs. Plus, you'd definitely remember it. Not to mention, it's a very handy and versatile plant. If you burn yourself on your oven or something, you can break a piece off and rub the aloe gel on your burn. You're welcome!

But the point is, you don't need a reason to give someone a gift. If you see something someone might like, go ahead and get it. No need to wait for a holiday. Get it and give it to them.

Then, if and when a special occasion day arrives and you didn't get them anything, you might still be OK because you have built your reputation for giving gifts on non-occasion days.

It's worth a shot, plus it feels really good to give gifts to people when they aren't expecting them.

Also, on the gift giving theme, I have a really good tip for you.

I don't know if this has ever happened to you before, but it happened to me and I wasn't prepared, so I found a solution and I've been good ever since. Here is the scenario.

Either there is some kind of occasion or not, but a friend or acquaintance arrives at your home and brings a gift. You smile and accept the gift, and it's a little awkward because you don't have a gift for them.

Here's what I do. While I'm out shopping or traveling in my day-to-day life, if I see something I think would be a cool gift, I buy it. I'll buy all types of cool potential gifts at different price levels.

I bring the items home and wrap them in a non-holiday-style wrapping paper and put a sticky note on the package saying what it is. Then I put the gifts in my closet.

When the scenario presents itself, and someone arrives with a gift for me, I say, "Ah, excellent! I have something for you, too!" and I go to the closet, look through the gifts, and pick out the appropriate one. Voila!

I have an assortment of blank greeting cards as well if I really want to go the extra mile with it.

This also comes in handy if you need a gift on short notice for a party or something. You just grab something from the stack.

You're welcome!

GIVE INVITES

Instead of just being focused on getting invites, it's good to give invites as well. So, like I mentioned earlier, I had a wine and cheese event at my apartment to meet neighbors and to invite people from other events. I try to think of activities I'm doing—I mentioned the street racing and things like that. I think, *Who would want to come to this?* And I will invite people who I think might enjoy doing what I'm about to do. That's another thing. When I talk about putting your interests out there, people need to know what you like so they know what to possibly invite you to.

I like street racing, so if I'm having a street racing event, I will invite everyone who I think would be interested in that. If I've met you at the symphony and you never expressed any interest in street racing, I would probably not invite you because I would think you wouldn't be interested. But anyone who had told me they're into that sort of thing, I'd think, *Oh, this person gets an invite.*

So, invite people to stuff you create or are interested in, and that's another great way to strengthen your relationship. Anytime you engage in an activity with somebody, it strengthens that relationship; you're bonding over the activity. Here in Colorado, axe throwing is becoming popular. There are places where you go and throw axes. The place by me requires a group of eight people to go do it, so it's a good opportunity for me to invite seven people to come with me.

Try to attend as many activities and host as many activities as you can, because it really takes you far, fast, on the social scene, and you'll get better each time you do it.

You already have a relationship with them. It might just be an acquaintance, but then maybe it'll be a strong acquaintance. Or maybe a light friend or solid friend, after you bond through a few of these experiences together. It's simply people out having a good time enjoying the event or activity. That's how friendships are built, right?

The more of these things you can attend (where it isn't you just standing around in a suit with some drinks talking about fundraising or something), the better. When you engage in an activity or some kind of hobby, it brings people together. So, don't be afraid to have your own events and invite people—don't just wait for people to invite you to things. Get that face-to-face time in.

IF YOU SAY YOU'RE GOING TO GO…

When people invite me, I always go, or…almost always. Here's how it works. A lot of times while I'm traveling, I meet new people, we hit it off, and they usually are from some other country than the one I am currently visiting. For example, they might say something like, "Come to Estonia. Meet me in Estonia. I'd like to show you around."

Then I say I'll go, because how often do you get invited to Estonia? And so, I'll go, stay with their family, they show me around, and it strengthens that relationship. If I say I'm going to go, I will go.

Here's a little story for you. I was on a sailing yacht with my brother and some friends, and it was a great time. The crew of the boat was really cool. One of the crew members invited my brother to go visit his country, Guyana, and my brother said, "Yes, I will go."

I said, "Don't say you're going to go if you're not going to go."

And he said, "Oh, no. I'll go. I'll go visit him."

And what do you suppose happened? After we were done sailing and got back to Denver, this person called my brother and said, "When are you thinking about coming, so we can get this on the calendar?"

My brother said, "Oh, yeah. I'm not going to go."

Then the person was like, "What? You said you were going to go."

And my brother said, "Oh, no, no. I have some scheduling issues."

I knew this was probably going to happen because people do this all the time. They say they're going to go and then don't go.

REMEMBER THIS! You *have* to go if you say you're going to go. The mistake my brother made was putting himself too far out of his social networking comfort zone and into a situation that...Well, I knew he wasn't going to do it, and I think he knew he wasn't going to do it. I think he'd like to imagine himself doing it. But he didn't do it. So that friendship and connection he could have had died right there. He killed it.

The guy who invited him was a pretty cool guy. He didn't invite ME, though. He invited my brother. If my brother would have gone, he would have had the experience of meeting that person in his home country, in his hometown, been shown around, see what they do. Get the feel of the local flavor, what's going on there, and meet new people, expanding his network into that area and into that new country. He'd potentially have made a new friend for life.

When you go and visit someone like that, it tends to build a very strong connection. I imagine they'd still be friends and that person might have come and visited him in return. My brother would have had the foundation set with that person and a new city. But since he didn't, all of it died.

So, don't make that mistake.

If someone invites you and you know you're not going to go, don't say you're going to go. If someone invites you and you say you're going to go, go. You must go. Don't complain about not being able to expand your network or missing out on great opportunities if you don't show up. Don't let my brother's mistake be your mistake. Go if you say you're going to go.

MAKE INTRODUCTIONS

Once you start going to events, hosting events, and inviting people, you start becoming known. Earlier we talked about "the walkthrough." Once you're known, you can do the walkthrough, and it will feel really good.

You want to get to a certain level of being known, but there's always going to be other circumstances where you're not known, especially if you go to another country, or if you go into another category of interest because, like I said, a lot of these things overlap, but then there'll be a whole new category of something that doesn't overlap with the others, so now you're not known anymore. You're only known in these circles, but you're not known over here.

When you find yourself in a new situation, you always go back to the basics, start over, and build it the same way. The more you do it, the better you'll be at it and the faster you'll be able to do it. Let's say you reach a point where you have a nice level of being known. You are going to want to use your position to make introductions.

This is what networking is all about. If you know somebody who's like, "Hey, Nick, I'm working on this project and I've gone through a bunch of computer programmers. They're always really shady, and the ones I find always rip me off." If I know somebody who can help them..."I know someone who has a reputation for being a really good programmer, highly recommended with references," or, "I know this guy. He's been good to me. I can send him your way. I can give you the contact information," or, "I know somebody who would know that."

Perhaps somebody says, "I'm trying to get in shape. I need a good personal trainer." I could say, "Oh. I know two really good personal trainers. What exactly are you looking for? I will run it by both of them if you want, and we can see who might be a good fit, and then I can put them in contact with you."

Introductions are GOLD.

As you meet people, you'll find out what their projects are, what their interests are, and they might hit a snag some-where someday. If you should happen to know somebody who specializes in whatever that snag is, you can say, "Oh, maybe this person," and you're just making the intro, so you're not saying they have to use this person. You just say, "This person is interested in this and maybe you two should get together because I think there can be a value exchange. This person may be able to help you out with your project."

A lot of people have introduced me that way. When I hit a snag in a project, I express what I'm trying to do or find to my network.

Most of the time, someone will respond and say, "I know somebody who does that."

I'm paying attention, I'm actively listening, so if I hear some-one has an issue and I think I know someone who might be able to help, I think, *Is there an introduction I can make?*

And when I do it, I don't keep score. You're not trying to say, "Well I did this for you so now you owe me."

No. You're just giving. You're just putting the goodwill out there, building good karma. You're trying to help as many people as you can. So, with your connections, you have the responsibility to use them for the greatest good and try to add as much value as you can.

If I can personally help somebody out, I will. I just help them. I say, "Here, here, here. This is for you. It seemed like you needed help with this. Feel free to use it or not. But I'm trying to add some value to your thing," or, "I wrote some ideas down that might help you. Feel free to use them if they prove to be helpful."

"You know I'm just thinking about this thing you're doing; you were looking for this, and I found this," or, "I was day-dreaming in traffic about your problem, and I came up with these. Feel free to use them or not."

It's nice when people are thinking about you and trying to help you out.

Sometimes people will return the favor and do it for you, sometimes they won't, but don't expect people to do it. Just you do your part. This is all part of the balance of maintaining relationships. You're all looking out for each other. You're a family. You're a gang. You all have each other's backs. You need to do your part. If they don't do theirs, then that's on them. But you do your part, step up, and be as good a person as you can be for your network. You be the example.

IN THE ROOM, IN THE DEAL

This is a saying. At any given moment, there is business

going on, deals being formed and worked through, and some will turn out to be very lucrative. These happen long before they make it into your newspaper or go public on the stock exchange. How do people find out about these things? Simple: in the room, in the deal.

If you have built a network of people who are action takers, people who are constantly pushing the boundaries, you will most likely be invited to early rounds of fundraising for startup companies.

So, when you are making your rounds, you say, "What are you working on?"

And they say, "I'm doing this project."

You might say, "Wow! That sounds fascinating."

"Well, I'm going to raise some money for whatever."

"I want to get in on that."

They might not offer, but then again, they might.

Or you might say, "If you are raising money one day for that project, I would like to get in on that."

So occasionally you will be able to get in on certain deals

that are not necessarily available to other people or at least not available at such an early stage. You might have the opportunity to get in on the ground floor of something big, you never know.

I have been presented with opportunities this way simply because I happened to be there and asked the right questions about a project.

Through your network, when people are talking about their projects, if something interests you, you might have an opportunity to get in on it. It might work out, or it might not, but you were there at the beginning.

You have to know people and be known by people. If you're known and trusted, they'll share all kinds of things with you. But you have to be there. You have to be connected, and that's why you're reading this book: to use these principles to be in the room and in the deal.

ENHANCED NETWORKING

So, once you actually get the ball rolling and you've met enough people that you're somewhat known, you can do enhanced networking. For example, I got invited to a Christmas party, and I didn't want to go.

Several people told me, "You need to go. You have to go."

So, I went, and I wasn't expecting to stay long because I was really tired and was planning on going to bed early that night.

Shortly after I showed up, one of my friends approached and said, "You have to meet this person," and introduced me to a very remarkable woman.

She said, "Hey, Nick, I've heard about you...everyone was talking about you earlier, and I really wanted to meet you."

Then my friend who made the introduction handed me a drink. "Here's an old-fashioned." Bam! I liked old-fashioneds (and Manhattans, too, so you know for future reference).

So...I had an old-fashioned in hand and a worldly, intriguing woman engaging me in great conversation. Later, some other friends came by and more introductions to new people were made.

I didn't have to try to actively network. Friends were bringing people over to meet *me*. That's what I call enhanced networking because I didn't really have to do anything. I just had to show up, which goes back to our initial main principle: SHOW UP. I simply showed up. Everything fell into place. Naturally, that doesn't happen all the time, but it happens often enough. If you put down a good foundation in your networking, you can expect an "enhanced network-ing" situation to happen from time to time.

I was so happy I went to that party. I had a really great time. It shows you what's possible when you show up, put in the work, and maintain your relationships. These things build on each other.

So, I'm encouraging you—even if you don't want to go—go, show up, and put in the work. Keep the light shining on your relationships, and these things can happen. I was able to get a lot of value and give a lot of value that evening. Now, when I go to other events, I see people I met from that night. We greet each other, catch up, and find ways to help each other in our projects. Good stuff!

That's a really good place to be, and you can get there very quickly, a lot faster than you imagine, but you have to put in the work to build and maintain the relationships.

HOW ARE YOU INTRODUCED?

Here's a very interesting and valuable thing I learned. It's how people introduce you.

Notice how people introduce you. So, as you attend events, pay attention to how the people you know introduce you to their friends and colleagues.

You will notice different people introduce you in different ways.

The way you're introduced is how that person sees you and what they feel is the most interesting thing about you. So, they might say, "This is Nick. He is an environmental specialist," and so they think that is the most interesting thing about me to tell this other person. They might say, "This is Nick, the 'connected introvert.' He teaches people how to network."

"This is Nick. He does crazy street racing, but I'm sure he stays within the bounds of the law and races safely."

"This is Nick. He's shooting an interesting documentary in Brazil."

So, it just depends on what they think is really interesting about you and what they think the person they are introducing you to will find most interesting.

The way you're being introduced is going to be what shapes the first impression this new person will have of you.

I find this very intriguing because people can get pretty creative at times. Usually, people pick from how they know you, what they think is fascinating about you, and their experiences with you. They'll pick out something, and when they refer to you, they refer to you as *X*, whatever this thing is that they find fascinating.

So, you might think you should be introduced a certain way, but that might not be the case.

Usually in that regard, they know the other person most likely finds a certain thing interesting, and so after the introduction, they're going to want me to lead off in my conversation with a topic related to how they introduced me.

So, if they introduce me as their former English as a Second Language teacher in Japan, I'm not going to start off the conversation about how I was swimming and almost drowned in the Caribbean trying to impress a girl. Instead, I'll start off talking about my days as an English teacher and the challenges and adventures I faced during that time, because that's how I was introduced. And this might be the connecting factor that I'm going to have with this new person. So, you'll always want to pay attention...and you will get a good vibe on how people see you by how they introduce you. So always pay attention to how you're introduced.

So when you're introduced in a certain way, lead off with however you're introduced, and then you can try to fill out some other things, ask questions, be an active listener, and then transition into something else if you want.

DIPLOMATIC EATING

While you are building your network and connecting with people, there is a high chance that at some point you will have to do some diplomatic eating.

Diplomatic eating is when you eat food you would normally never eat but now find yourself in a situation where you have to eat it to not insult your host.

Let me give you two examples of when this happened to me.

I was in Japan and went to a birthday party of a friend. There were two Americans there, including me, and two people from Spain. Everyone else at the party was Japanese. Nothing particularly noteworthy happened until it was time to eat. Now, what I'm accustomed to in the United States is a buffet-style dinner, meaning, you have a plate and you serve yourself. You put the items on your plate yourself in the quantity you desire. However, in Japan, at least at this house, they bring your plate out, and it has what you're going to eat on it.

They brought my plate out and set it in front of me. It had two large octopus tentacles, two large squid tentacles, fried pumpkin, and something in a little orange pile that I couldn't identify. I politely asked, gesturing to the pile with a smile, "What might this be?" The reply was "Crab eggs."

Crab eggs!? What!? Who eats crab eggs? I never knew that

was a thing! Also, although I enjoy octopus and squid, I was used to having them in a much smaller form, not giant tentacles with suction cups as big as dimes on them, sitting on my plate. So...yep, you guessed it. I kicked in my diplomatic eating.

I looked over at the other American and the Spanish couple, and they were digging in and eating with delight and big smiles. So, I was not going to be the one that punks out.

The trick is to eat fast and imagine that the meal is something you really like, but it's disguised in the form of something else to try to throw you off.

I grabbed those tentacles, dipped them in soy sauce, and ate them like I hadn't eaten in days. I scooped up the crab eggs and shoveled them in my mouth, followed up with the pumpkin, smiling the whole time and exclaiming, "Oishii!" (delicious).

I was so proud of myself, I leaned back in my chair to bask in my victory. The hostess was also impressed and happy I enjoyed it. So happy, in fact, that she brought me another plate with the same items and portion size.

I smiled and thanked her. However, on the inside I was screaming, "No-o-oo!"

I took a deep breath and repeated the process. Dunked the tentacles, shoveled the crab eggs, and followed up with nice, palate-cleansing fried pumpkin. And another "Oishii!"

This time I patted my belly and let the host know it was delicious but I was way too full to have another serving.

So. Chalk up a victory for ol' Nick! The lesson learned that day was, yes, eat fast, but don't eat too fast and don't be too happy about it.

The next example takes place in Nicaragua. I was having dinner with a family one evening. Their home was quite large, and so it had a courtyard with an open ceiling right next to the kitchen and dining area.

We were seated at a long rectangular table that could comfortably seat about fourteen people, however, there were only five of us there.

For some reason, I was seated at the head of the table and the two women and two children I was dining with sat at the other end of the table, so we weren't grouped together. I was...over "here."

Anyway, the woman of the house served my plate, and it looked absolutely delicious. Tortillas, shredded chicken, beans, and rice. No problem, right?

One of the children decided he was going to have some fun, and I believe he threw a bean at his sister. She screamed. The two women of the house were not going to put up with his nonsense, so they started disciplining him.

While this was going on and their attention was on him, a large bird flew in from the open courtyard ceiling and shit on my head and my plate of food.

I started laughing, because of course this would happen to me, and I grabbed my napkin to wipe off my head.

I stopped laughing when I realized that nobody saw that happen, nobody knew about the bird shit. At the time, my Spanish wasn't good enough to adequately explain what had happened.

The ladies finished fussing with the kid, turned to me, gestured to my plate, and said, "Eat!"

My heart sank.

I looked over to the stove and saw there was no additional food over there. If I were to somehow explain what happened, one of the women would probably have given me her plate, but then, what was she going to eat?

I dug deep on this one. I looked down at my plate and saw

the bird had been victorious in getting its signature on pretty much every part of my meal.

What do you figure I did?

I'll tell you what I did. Diplomatic eating. I stirred the excrement into my food and ate it. To be honest, you really couldn't taste it in there; it sort of blended in. Plus, once again, I ate fast.

Afterward, I excused myself and decided I needed to wrap up my evening and go lie down to wait for the consequences of my actions to kick in.

I thought, *Is this going to be how I die?*

But nothing happened. I was fine.

Now, I'm not saying you have to eat bird shit. I'm simply saying that sometimes you have to do a little diplomatic eating to keep things running smoothly in your circles.

SUMMARY

All right, let's review. You're going to want to make a list. Make a list of all the people in your phone, work email, and personal email contacts. Go through all of those people, and if you have a little black book or something, go through that too. Go through all the people and make a list of everyone you have not talked to recently whom you need to touch base with, and find a way to either see them face-to-face, which is the best way, or catch up by phone call, email, handwritten letter, or a video. I like to send videos. You need to reach out and touch base with these people. Do it. Maintain those relationships.

Use discretion. Once you are talking with people, they are going to share stuff with you, and you will share stuff with them. They are supposed to keep it to themselves, and you keep it to yourself.

Don't gossip about stuff people share with you. They are confiding in you; you're building trust. Trust is the foundation for building relationships, so you need to do your part and exercise discretion.

Be humble and honest. If you're invited somewhere and can't go because it's financial or something else is holding you back from going, just tell them, "I can't afford that," or, "I got someone pregnant, and I've got to deal with that." You know, whatever it is. *This is just an example, by the way; I didn't get anyone pregnant.*

But whatever it is, just tell people what happened, and it's much better than saying, "Oh, it's a scheduling conflict." Just tell them. Tell them, and it might open up another bonding thing because they might be able to relate with whatever you're going through.

Gift giving: you don't need a reason to give someone a gift. Do it anytime you find something you think they would like. Also...it's nice to have some extra gifts handy that are prewrapped at your house, so you are ready for any surprise or quick occasions.

Make introductions. If you know somebody would be interested in meeting someone else, or if you think that someone could benefit from the help of somebody, make the introduction. Someone has a skill and this person over here needs that skill. Offer to make that introduction.

You can ask both sides, "Would it be OK if I introduce you to this person who has this skill?" or, "This person is looking for this. Would it be OK if I drop your name for that?" And just make the introduction to help them both because they might not otherwise be able to meet or even know that the person has that skill. But you can make that introduction and add value.

Add value without keeping score. Add as much value to your network as you can. Whenever you can help somebody out, just help them out and don't be like, "Well, I helped you twice and you only helped me once, so you have to catch up." None of that. Just help them, add value, keep moving forward, and maybe some of that will come back around another way. You never know. But do your part.

You be the first mover. Take action first. Step up.

There used to be a time when I felt I would like it if more people would say Happy Birthday to me on my birthday because it doesn't happen that often. And when other people's birthdays came around, I would think, *I don't know if I should say Happy Birthday to them because they didn't say Happy Birthday to me.* But then I thought, *You know what, let me just do it. Let me be the one. It doesn't matter what they do. I'm going to give them what I myself would like, no strings attached.*

I don't care if they say it to me, I'm going to be the one. I will step up and say it. I will say Happy Birthday to you on your birthday (if I remember). I will be the first mover, and I'll do it. If you don't do it, that's fine. I'm going to do my part. I've never regretted doing that. I will give the person what I would like someone to do for me, and they might not do it back, but at least I'm going to give them the experience I wish I had. I think it's a good habit. Be a good friend.

In the room, in the deal: a lot of times, there are cool opportunities that happen, but you have to be around to know they are happening to possibly be included in them. So with networking, if you play your cards right, if you're a likable person and are maintaining your relationships, you may have opportunities to be involved in different investments, opportunities, or experiences you normally wouldn't be. Most people don't get access to these opportunities because they're not there. You're there, so you might get to participate in a lot of cool stuff that you otherwise wouldn't.

Enhanced networking: after you've put in the work and you're somewhat known, it's easier to network because people will introduce more and more people to you. So, your networking requires less effort because it's enhanced from other people who know you already.

There will still be places where it's not the case, because you went outside your normal circle and opened up some new circles, but there are going to be certain times when it is very much enhanced and you just have to show up. Then the magic can happen simply by you being there.

Notice how you're introduced. I cannot stress how important it is to pay attention to how people introduce you because, once again, they are giving you an insight into what they think is interesting about you or what they think is going to be interesting about you to the person they're introducing you to. So, you're going to want to lead off with how you were introduced.

That gives you a conversation starter to kick it off. So just be mindful of that because it can help you know what some people think your strengths are at least for this particular situation. So be aware of it.

Diplomatic eating: sometimes—actually probably more times than you would expect—you will have to do some diplomatic eating to save face and not disrespect your host(ess). So, eat fast, compliment, and tell yourself that this is food you like disguised as food you don't care for. This is a great talent to develop and will serve you well.

Chapter Nine

THE BIG REVIEW

Hooray! You pretty much finished the book, so congratulations! If you apply these things, it's going to work for you. Let me know how it works, reach out, touch base with me, and let me know how it's going. I've seen a lot of success with this, and a lot of people I have coached have done some really incredible things using these techniques. If you go through the steps, you are going to see results, and you're going to see them faster than you expect. But you have to put in the work. So, to hit some of the main points:

Nothing happens until you show up. You need to show up more than you think. A lot of times you won't want to. I'm an introvert. I like being at home. I like not going out, but I still show up because I know if I don't, nothing is going to happen.

Get pre-known if you can. If you can, get on the online chat group and get pre-known, or if before the event, someone says they want to meet up for beers, go. Or you can be *that* person and say, "I'm going to be here the day before or the morning before the event to have breakfast or whatever. Who wants to meet me?" Do it because it will really give you a leg up in meeting people and getting some quality time with them before the event starts. It's great to try to get pre-known as much as possible before an event.

Be early. Remember, if you're early, you can get the lay of the land, and you'll have more control. As people are coming in, you can see where you want to be situated. You can get all of your ducks in a row, so to speak. You just have more power if you're there early and can observe the flow and set yourself up for success.

Duke Cookie Face. This is probably the most important thing in this book. This has served me well. Every day I use this, and I am just amazed at how well it works. So be sure to add this to your arsenal of things. Use Duke Cookie Face—it is a miracle worker. I expect to hear back from you on what it's done for you when you use it. It is incredible. I cannot say enough about this technique.

The Magic of Three. Remember you want to get three going. That's a perfect number for networking. If you already have a plus-one with you, you're going to need to snag one more person. Then try to break off and leave those two. They're going to make the group of three with someone else, and you go make a new three-person group. You always want to get that three. So, if you're hunting introverts, grab one and start talking to them. Grab another one, and you have your three. It gives you more flexibility and helps the conversation go much more smoothly.

Observations, questions, and stories. That's what you talk about. People always ask, "Well, what do I say? What do I say?" And there are a lot of books, plenty of books, that have icebreakers and conversation starters. You don't have to memorize all that stuff. Just use observations, questions, and stories. So, you observe, see what's going on, and make a comment. "What do you think about that?" "Look at that. What about that thing?" "I noticed..."

Ask questions. "What's with that belt?" "What's going on there?" "Did you see that?" "I thought they were going to have food, but there's no food." And then tell stories. If you have a story that somehow fits and is going to be applicable to the situation, tell your short story. Keep it streamlined and smooth. Don't bore anyone with some long, drawn-out story with no good punch line. But tell your story if it fits.

So, observations, questions, and stories. If you just remember that, you will always have something to say because you just have to notice something and say it. And then question.

You ask a question either about something you noticed or about something they said. You can just pick something out of their sentence and ask a question about it. And if that reminds you of a story, tell the story. Boom!

Add value. Remember, you are not keeping score. Anytime you see that you can add value to somebody in some situation, add value. If you need to make an introduction, do that. Or if you can just help that person, do it.

If you see someone struggling in an uncomfortable situation, add value or a helping hand. You never know where it might lead.

Discretion. Don't gossip. As you're making connections and gaining people's trust, they are going to be vulnerable around you. They are trusting you with certain information, certain scenarios. You need to be a friend, a confidant, and not go blabbing to other people about it. Hold yourself accountable and responsible. If you want to build a strong network, you need to learn how to keep your mouth shut. It's a matter of trust.

Maintain your relationships. Once again, after you build these relationships, it's best to try to meet as many people face-to-face as possible. But if you can't, then somehow get in touch with them at least quarterly. Go through all your contacts in your phone, computer, your work email, personal email, and just reach out to the people. See what they are doing. See what they're up to because you never know. But you need to keep these things fresh because you put in all the time to build these relationships, and you've got to maintain them. Otherwise you'll lose everything you've gained.

Remember, you are only ONE connection away from stepping into your destiny, and it all starts by simply showing up.

Before this moment, you couldn't go "ALL IN" because you didn't know what to do. And now you DO know what to do so...it's possible.

I find that, for me, knowledge in and of itself isn't quite enough to get me there. There is a little something extra that makes a BIG difference.

I needed to let someone believe in me.

When that happened, it was the final piece of the puzzle. Everything fell into place.

I can tell you this: I may not know you, but I believe in you. I honestly do. I believe that with these techniques you can, and will, do great things.

I'm already proud of you for reading this book. That was step one.

Step two is applying what you've learned.

These skills will take you places you never imagined!

I believe in you.

Your new life awaits. I'll see you on the yacht!

~Nick Shelton

P.S. For more information or to find out how you can work with me, check out www.connectedintrovert.com.

ACKNOWLEDGMENTS

First and foremost, I would like to thank James Trapp, who was my accountability buddy through this process to make sure I did what I said I was going to do and do it within the time frame I was supposed to do it in. Without him, this book would not have come out when it did...or ever.

I want to thank my brother, Jason Shelton, who pushed me to write this book so that I may add more value to the world of introverts. I take my brother for granted a LOT but am very grateful to have him in my life.

And to Shane Barone, who was an eager and early student of mine and who became a good friend. Thank you for supporting the mission, the process, and me as I shine my light into the world.

To all of my friends, colleagues, and associates. I hope your dreams are amazing and that you see them come to pass.

ABOUT THE AUTHOR

NICK SHELTON, "the connected introvert," has been fine-tuning the craft of effective, high-level social strategy and networking for twenty years. Beginning with his time in the United States Air Force, Nick learned skills that were indispensable to his journey. Coupled with extensive research and fifteen years of experience in the oil and gas industry, Nick finally "cracked the code" and developed tools that gave him the confidence to flourish in social situations.

Nick has successfully built a strong, international network of friends, colleagues, and associates and continues to teach introverts how to navigate social events with ease. You can learn more about Nick—and his methods—at www.connectedintrovert.com.